HEAL TO LEAD

Raven + Grace

Contents

A Gift From the Authors

Throughout this book, we've shared powerful tools and practices that have guided us on our healing journeys, empowering us to lead with strength and purpose. Now, we want to extend these resources to you.

We've created a collaborative digital workbook to accompany this book, filled with valuable tools to support your own journey. Inside, you'll find journal prompts to help you gain clarity, guided meditations to nurture your soul, and transformational educational videos designed to inspire your growth. To download, visit https://ravenand-grace.com/healtolead2.

It's our hope that these resources will enrich your experience and support you on your path to healing and leadership.

With heartfelt gratitude,
The Authors of Heal to Lead

HEAL TO LEAD

Introduction

THEA SOMMER

HEAL: Become sound or healthy again.

LEAD: Be a route or means of access to a particular place or in a particular direction.

A great and challenging way of living is being able to turn around fast enough to see yourself. And then, there's the incredible gift of helping others do that for themselves.

Being invited to write a chapter for *Heal to Lead: Stories to Turn Your Wounds Into Wisdom, Volume One* was thrilling for me. Being asked to write the introduction for this volume is such an honor.

I've been in the personal development field for four decades as a program leader, facilitator, coach, and trainer of coaches. I would say that the most important perspective I have is that people really do want to be their best selves.

In this type of transformational work and leadership, there is empowering others to achieve success and there is continually doing courageous work on oneself.

Heal To Lead: Stories to Turn Your Wounds Into Wisdom, Volume Two is an incredible collection of leaders sharing about their own healing journeys and the impact it has made on their lives and the lives of others.

If you're interested in your own growth and development and/or empowering others, you're in the right spot. The vulnerability and authenticity of these stories is beyond inspiring.

"I have come to the frightening conclusion that I am the decisive element.

It is my personal approach that creates the climate.

It is my daily mood that makes the weather.

I possess tremendous power to make life miserable or joyous.

I can be a tool of torture or an instrument of inspiration. I can humiliate or humor, hurt or heal.

In all situations, it is my response that decides whether a crisis is escalated or de-escalated, and a person is humanized or de-humanized.

If we treat people as they are, we make them worse.

If we treat people as they ought to be, we help them become what they are capable of becoming."

- Goethe

One

On the Verge

Step Beyond the Beliefs

PATRICIA H. SIMMS

W hen I was young, younger than I can almost remember, my mom would take my older sister and me to the large wall-size window that occupied the dining room of our home in Montreal. She would draw two enormous dining chairs from the table and place them inches away from the window. My sister would find her way to one and mom would sit in the other, offering her lap to me with a welcoming smile. We would sit together and stare out to the horizon and she would ask us what we saw.

BLOWING OUT THE SUN

On this particular late winter afternoon, I remember asking why the trees were all empty. She smiled and paused, holding her thoughts. I could feel her breath as her belly moved in and out, and felt a calm-

1

ing sensation simmer in my bones. We sat there and watched, our eyes searching for a sign that something was about to change. Then it came into view...what we were waiting for. The sun began to set and we caught the first glimpse of it as it descended below the top of our window frame. It was bright and bold and full of fire. It was fearless and full of energy. And it was then that, through the shadows, I began to see life.

I fidgeted to see more. Mom reminded me to sit and watch, for the best was yet to come. I glanced at my sister sitting in her elusive stillness, so I sat too. It was in this moment, with the present awareness of a four-year-old, yet the deep generational understanding in my soul, I witnessed the vastness of space between us and the sun, and the radiating warmth projected through the window. I witnessed the moment between day and night and it was this time when all things were possible. We sat there until the sun was but only a glint of radiant light, and we counted down from ten and blew out the sun.

This became a ritual for us, and we would eventually leave the chairs facing the window. Over a year later on the eve of a late spring night, we sat in our chairs waiting to blow out the sun. Mom told us the sun did not set but rather the Earth moved and everything changed in every moment. I noticed the flowers on the trees had fallen and leaves now dressed the branches. Mom also shared that change was inevitable; every season had a purpose, and the way we looked at things would define how we see ourselves. I came to realize that on the days we weren't able to sit in our chairs and blow out the sun, that the sun would set anyways. I had no idea what she was talking about as I barely surpassed my toddler years, but her words found their way into the fibers of my being and have guided my path as I travel the journey of my life.

BECAUSE I LOOK LIKE HER

As I grew older, our evening ritual faded. What replaced it was the ritual of hearing heavy footsteps up to the bedroom I shared with my sister. My heart pounded as I pretended to sleep. I could hear my father open the door and call my name. I learned to be still and quiet so as to not alert him that I still might be awake. The hauling me out of bed to empty my half-full trash can while yelling and slinging insults, thankfully, would be delayed for another night because on this night, he turned away and closed the door just enough to reveal the hall light witnessing this repetitive nightly scene. Growing up in a home filled with deep layers of dysfunction embedded by the traumatic years my father spent in the Lodz Ghetto during the early years of Nazi occupied Poland, followed by a year behind the barbed wire fences of Auschwitz, fell heavy on our family.

Know that I took the brunt of it.

Because I looked like her.

I was named after her.

I was her in my father's eyes.

His mother, Helen.

As much as he loved me, as much as he loved her, the guilt of leaving her that night in 1938 when he, his brother, and father fled the over-crowded ghetto apartment was something that encompassed him. She was very ill and could not escape with them, so they left her behind, hearing the shots fired as they fled. Every time he looked at me, I was the reminder. His grief, his torment and anguish, his anger and hatred consumed him every day he survived.

Through all his suffering I suffered. I was his pride and joy, yet I was his misery. I was strong and capable, yet paralyzed with constant fear. My survival became his distraction; I entertained him, kept him busy, but it was never enough. I stayed close and tried to comfort him by playing the role of all the things that were taken from his young life. I became the caretaker, the fixer, the mediator; and, even in my strength and courage, I became his guilt and shame.

I remember lying in bed one night after a challenging dinner with dad, and mom came in to say good night. She sat on the edge of my bed and kissed my forehead. She was sad. I could always feel her sadness, and at this moment, I asked her to leave him. She looked deeply into my child-self and said, "I can't. He's been through so much in his life that if I left and took you kids, it would break him."

This moment has been emblazoned in my being both from a place of shock and anger. I remember the toll it took when she surrendered herself, her desires, her autonomy. It was the moment she decided his life was more important than hers. It was the moment she decided he got to live and she didn't. She died of curable stage 1 breast cancer at the age of sixty-five. I had no idea that thirty-plus years in the future I would almost replicate this moment.

I AM NOT WILLING TO DIE FOR YOU

Studies have shown that cycles repeat themselves, so it was not surprising I found a partner who suffered deep trauma from the moment of conception. He suffered grief and loss within days of his birth when he was placed in a Catholic orphanage until he was adopted. His adoptive father was both mentally and physically abusive to the family, but especially to him being the first child and a boy. This led to great shame, and the addiction to alcohol and drugs created a band-aid to numb this agony. All this unbeknownst to me, I chose him. I saw what I wanted to see and what I was searching for after a myriad of dysfunctional and oftentimes abusive relationships. He promised not to be like the others, and honestly, we had no idea of the trauma he suffered until it surfaced following his catastrophic car accident, which triggered childhood memories of abuse.

Following his accident, the slow unraveling of our twenty-five-year marriage moved into high speed and crumbled. The marriage was challenged from the start: He was attracted to me for my strength, courage, determination, decisiveness, and confidence. What he loved about me he also hated. I found someone who was kind, passive, agreeable, and whom I could help and nurture. What I loved about him also frustrated me to no end. For the marriage to work, for him to feel loved and valued, I had to be the glue that held the broken pieces of his life together. Every time he looked at me, he felt love, but also resentment, which turned to shame. And it took a great toll. On the day I decided to end my marriage, I recall looking in the mirror, now one-hundred pounds overweight with increasing health issues, asking:

When did I become less important than him?

Why do I struggle so much to deeply love myself?

I also remember saying, "I am not willing to die for you."

It will be four years this August since I left my marriage and chose to put myself first. We tried to mend the relationship prior to me leaving, but his trauma was too much, and I could not be the pillar he needed to stand on any longer. Along with this decision, came incredible fear about the what ifs.

I was fifty-seven and leaving a long-term marriage, my beautiful home, my friends, my life. I was walking away from stability, familiarity, and security. It was 2020 and the world was living in the throes of the Covid-19 pandemic. Now, uncertainty was the only reality we knew. It was the most difficult decision I have ever made, but I did it to save myself. It was the only way to give myself the life I desired for decades. I put myself first and I left. I moved to another state, a new home, and started over.

My business of fifteen years had crumbled during the pandemic, and I was living mostly on credit cards and a business loan. After the short pity-party three months into my move, I sat down on my yoga mat and breathed. I came up with a plan. This plan began with sitting on my yoga mat every day and simply breathing.

It gave me time.

It gave me clarity

And it gave me peace that I longed for.

I sat and listened to my breath get calm and quiet. I journaled. Every day. Most days I didn't feel like writing, so I made a habit to write at least seven things I was grateful for. It helped.

What followed was pivotal in my ability to start over and create the version of myself I wanted. I faced beliefs that made up my identity for over half a century and squashed them by writing down evidence of why I'm not limited to those beliefs. It opened the door to shift my perspective. I regained the confidence to go back to school for another degree and multiple certifications to enhance my educational consulting business into the post-pandemic era of artificial intelligence, Zoom, and life coaching Gen Z and Millennials, helping them navigate the world of dream careers, and educational and employment opportunities. My mornings began with calm, lightness, creativity, and imagination, followed by purposeful hours both at my computer and in my garden.

LOVING MYSELF FIERCELY

I turned sixty in late winter of 2023 and enveloped myself into this new life. Success is revealed to me in each moment of everyday life, as are my obstacles and teachers. My evidence of a fulfilling life is the garden I planted that comes back each spring bearing fragrant blooms, vegetables, and fruit. It's the birds, squirrels, and even honey bees that come and drink from the fountain I made from two large boulders I found in the tattered backyard of my new home. It's the referral calls I receive from prospective clients looking for guidance and inspiration. It's the friendships foraged from a love of dogs and the great outdoors. It's the belly laughter shared between sisters. And, it is the loving relationship I have with my son.

Yes, I remember this moment. The moment so long ago when my sister and I would blow out the sun, as a reminder of all things possible. It was this in-between time that we could see more clearly. This in-between time when we felt the changing of seasons, the day into night, life into death and into life again. It's all on the verge, the verge of all things possible and a place where life keeps moving forward.

Now fifty-five years later and twenty-four years after the death of my mom, I continue to find my truth and my clarity when on the verge. It is this place, the place that changes your beliefs from impossible to I'm possible and trusting this is where growth can occur. It is in letting go of what we trust as true and stepping out to embrace the unknown, constantly shifting our perspective as we experience life. It is in the pushing through of a bud that turns into a bloom when the beautiful yet challenging experience occurs. We can call these experiences our teachers, all of them!

On occasion, I still find myself relying on old beliefs, challenging myself to keep plodding forward, doing more, and thinking it will lead me to a place where I can do less. I sometimes feel myself changing and hoping for a significant feeling of contentment. I strive to be happy, as if this was something tangible and within reach.

That first day I blew out the sun, spring was on the verge. Today I can feel it just beyond my gaze, beyond my fingertips. I can smell it through the space between the chill that lingers and the warmth the fiery sun breathes right through me.

On my yoga mat, half moon is on the verge,
hip peeling open feeling one stack over the other,
the broadness across my chest expanding with clarity,
and the ever-present standing leg, shaking and pleading for my breath to go deeper and longer.
My life is on the verge...
On the verge of greatness, yet on the verge of losing it all...
On the verge of falling in love, yet on the verge of falling apart...
On the verge of breaking out, yet on the verge of crawling in...
On the verge of knowing it all, yet on the verge of knowing nothing...

As I stand in each moment, I feel the balancing point wavering on the edge of profound fearlessness so I might feel the simplicity of grace beneath my feet.

Two

Two Wedding Dresses

Redefining My Life from Trauma to Freedom

MELISSA BUCHANAN

We all want to be loved and accepted. From an early age, we are implicitly or explicitly told how to act, think, and feel, that tries to define who we are in this world if we let it.

Some childhoods are built on playgrounds; mine was built on survival. Before the age of ten, my memories are a blur. My childhood was spent primarily alone with my mother, who was consumed by her addictions to sex, drugs, and male attention. I had no friends, nothing of my own (I even wore her clothes), and the last place I remember sleeping was on an apartment couch because my bed was filled with cockroaches. The only refuge I found was playing in the apartment dumpster down an alley. It was surrounded by a concrete casing and provided a space where I could hide that brought a sense of relief. I was still alone, but somehow when I was there, I felt safe.

My dad would pick me up every other weekend, often from who knows where. Visiting him was like entering a different world with his family—my stepmother, brother, and sister—a stark contrast to the chaos and violence I experienced with my mother. I appreciated the consistency of their household. Each night we gathered for family dinners, shared Saturday chores, and attended church on Sundays.

The peace at their house was fleeting, knowing I'd soon return to my mother's, where any sense of stability quickly faded away. Eventually, she finally agreed to let me move in with my dad and his family full-time. She had reached a stage where she could no longer maintain a place for herself, much less for me. Little did I know it would be one of the last times I would see her before her choices led her to move across the country in order to escape the law.

Once I moved in with my dad, I learned quickly how to play the "good girl" game. Attending church taught me acceptance came from following rules and one's value was measured by sacrificing oneself for others. Feeling like an outsider for so long as a child, I was determined to do whatever it took to fit in, marking the start of a long journey where I believed my worth was tied to my actions rather than who I was. I developed an intense fear that people would abandon me—after all, if my own mother couldn't be there for me, why would anyone else? Getting love meant molding myself into the perfect image of whoever the person in front of me wanted. I couldn't risk acknowledging my own desires, fearing they would make me stand out and tie me to my mother.

I held on to this outlook until my twenties, when I fell for a pastor's son from Alabama. Completely enamored with him, I was initially terrified by his desire to know the real me. I tried to deflect his attention elsewhere, but ultimately, I chose to let him in and give him a chance.

Not only did he love me, but his family embraced me as well. They lived in a charming house where we created constant memories filled with music, laughter, and delicious food. Weekends were spent around bonfires, sharing heartfelt conversations, and every corner of their home resonated with comfort and genuine warmth.

Despite the love they gave, my past creeped back in, overshadowing their frequent attempts to express how wonderful they thought I was. They saw beyond my "good girl" facade, but I struggled to believe them, fearing it would challenge the way of life I had maintained up to that point. As a result of this internal conflict, he proposed and I called off the wedding just one month before the date.

It took years to see that, regardless of the time I spent with them, my panic was quietly growing. Their presence made me question everything—my identity, the meaning of love—leaving me overwhelmed and paralyzed. Confronting my mother's neglect, the invisibility of my needs, and the idea that I could be seen for who I was alone felt daunting and almost unnatural to face. Instead, I fixated on doubting their affection, reinforcing the damaging beliefs I had internalized.

Even with traumatic upbringings, we often cling to familiar patterns and resist anything that challenges our established worldview. I was unaware of childhood trauma's effects, believing something was inherently flawed in me and I should always be doing more. This led to cycles of self-blame and relentless pressure, preventing me from seeking support and discovering new possibilities. Healing begins with understanding our roots to unravel deep-seated beliefs and perceptions. Avoiding the past can keep us stuck, perpetuating harmful and old programming.

CONFRONT LOSSES AND RELEASE THE REST

"Grief is an unexpected ally. Though we may fear it, grief often validates our experiences and reveals what truly matters to us."

Returning home felt like a strange rewind, drifting through job changes, unhealthy relationships, and cross-country travel, searching for solace while grappling with a deep sense of aimlessness. Burning bridges to return to what I knew only led to more confusion and disorientation. My identity, shaped by past traumas and self-imposed rules, left me unsure of who I was or which direction to take. The path ahead was clouded with uncertainty, and I knew there had to be another way, but I was at a loss for how to begin.

Then, the summer before I turned thirty, my life changed forever. I was setting up a Christmas in July party with friends when, in the midst of decorating, the phone rang. On the other end, a soft, loving voice—a family friend—delivered the devastating news: "Honey, your daddy died."

It was sudden and surreal. It didn't make sense; he was only fifty. How could this be? I had just spoken to him the day before.

I don't know what it's like to have a mental breakdown, but it feels like I was pretty close to that. Soon after the funeral, I went back to work but remained numb for many months, drifting in and out of reality to keep my internal world from crumbling. Over time, I found it difficult to concentrate at work, the inability to relax, and felt my tough exterior starting to crack under the weight of all I kept inside me.

For a long time, I couldn't see a death on TV or witness a father-daughter dance without feeling intense sadness. No matter how much we fight it, suppressed emotions will find their way out, even years later. Until they do, we often resort to extreme measures to avoid the hurt or become reactive when triggered. No one had told me about therapy, the complexities of grief, or that emotions are valid and okay. I didn't understand what it meant to process your feelings and instead admired my dad for his ability to hide his so well. I had mastered the art of ignoring, pushing through, and doing whatever it took to survive, believing anything else was a sign of weakness. It took learning through my next relationship—that healing requires facing pain head-on and embracing our feelings.

A couple years later, I met a sweet man through a mutual friend. He was a blue-collar worker with a tough history, yet a heart full of kindness. From the start, our connection felt magical, and I was drawn to how unconventional he seemed. He was funny, adventurous, and had an infectious zest for life. For two years, our love felt like a fairy tale—until it quickly unraveled.

Two short months after our wedding, it all came crashing down. He relapsed into a hidden drug addiction and became someone I no longer recognized. I vividly remember the moment I knew it was over—he was high, gaslighting me and insisting nothing was wrong. I realized I had married my mother and was now trying to rescue others, including him, while causing myself harm in the process. Following a period of rehabs, abuse, lies, and countless tears with no progress, I made the heartbreaking decision to ask for a divorce.

After this and my dad's passing, I hit rock bottom. I cried out to God, wondering if I was destined for a life of suffering, despite my efforts to be the person I thought I should be. My attempts to follow the "rules" weren't producing the results I had hoped for. Grief is a profound experience that touches everyone, yet it's hard to fully capture its depth. I couldn't navigate the pain alone like I had pretended to. Through therapy, I decided to confront it all and grief became a catalyst for change. It allowed me to fully feel, process, and accept my losses, ultimately leading to profound personal growth and closure.

Reflecting on both relationships, I came to understand the role of trauma in shaping my approach to love and intimacy. In my first relationship, I struggled to accept love. Intimacy terrified me, so I only revealed fragments of myself, hiding behind perfectionism and over-giving. I presented a version that fit others' expectations, keeping my true self hidden for safety and out of fear of rejection. Whenever my authentic self began to emerge, I would pull away, convincing myself I didn't need anyone. Trauma had turned my life into a constant game of strategy and survival.

By the time I entered my second relationship, I was more open to love but sought it from someone who couldn't love himself, let alone reciprocate it to me. I lacked boundaries, overlooked red flags, and had poor communication skills. With a focus on maintaining peace, I avoided conflict and blamed myself for problems, leading to one-sided relationships where I gave far more than I received without question.

To heal, I had to confront two truths: I had received pain, and I had caused it. Adulthood doesn't erase the influence of childhood trauma; instead, our past remains a close companion, shaping our identity, perceptions, and interactions. While trauma might have initially caused my mind to block out painful experiences for protection, it was now affecting how I related to the world, influencing my behaviors and thoughts.

True healing required me to face my story, validate what happened to me, and accept responsibility for the part I played. How I perpetuated unhealthy patterns, from failing to stand up for myself to hurting others and pushing them away. I was able to understand my own grief and shame, offering support to these emotions instead of running from them.

Forgiving and being honest with myself paved the way for extending forgiveness to others. I started focusing on what I could control—working on myself. This meant recognizing that people have the right to make their own choices, even if they differ from mine, and accepting it's alright to let go of those who can't meet my needs or choose not to change. Their path may be different, and that's okay.

Embracing this mindset shifted my perspective from reactive to introspective, empowering me to prioritize and pursue what aligned with who I wanted to be and what I wanted to be around. This new-found clarity opened doors that resonated with my values, helping me create a new path moving forward.

REDEFINE YOUR LIFE

"If we look at our lives through criticism, we will only see our failures. If we look through the lens of compassion, we will see our strengths and spark a future of healing."

Over the next two and a half years, I underwent profound growth. Focused on becoming a mental health therapist, I absorbed everything I could to learn about trauma's enduring impacts—its unseen scars on our emotional, mental, and physical health. I became passionate about freeing myself and others from its grip, which convinces us that we are defined by our past and have no other options.

I began envisioning the woman I wanted to become, and stepping into that felt right. I decided to launch a business and relocate to Nashville, a city I had always wanted to live in. I started to reimagine various aspects of my life, from crafting my ideal routine and discovering new hobbies to transforming my home into a sanctuary adorned with plants and filled with jazz music. Within a year, I was speaking on mental health panels, cultivating healthy relationships, and even meeting my current husband—a man I never knew existed. Rebuilding my life on my terms brought exhilaration and a rediscovery of countless joys from the little everyday moments to the big, life-changing experiences.

As a result, I coined the phrase "Redefine Your Life," creating a platform where clients can uncover their true desires, navigate through obstacles, and actively shape their future. It's been profoundly rewarding to witness them dismantle the walls they—or others—had carefully constructed over time, making room for new possibilities. I am thankful to walk alongside others with similar stories, offering insight and guidance, letting them know they are not alone. It is beautiful to see them step into lives characterized by authenticity and purpose.

Healing, especially from trauma, is a complex process that takes time. It's not something that can be easily undone or we should expect it to happen on its own or with a quick fix. It requires diligent effort and patience, often mirroring the years it took to build those wounds. Embracing compassion for ourselves, being open to change, questioning old narratives, and moving towards our goals are all essential.

The first step is to recognize recurring patterns in your life and consider their significance. Reflect on what triggers you and how these might provide insights into your identity, worldview, and unresolved issues from past traumas.

Next, acknowledge your role in shaping your story and take responsibility for your choices. Seek and offer forgiveness, especially toward yourself, while setting boundaries that nurture your well-being and healthier relationships.

As you move forward, envision your future self, values, and aspirations. Set clear goals, breaking down big obstacles into smaller, manageable steps to maintain focus and motivation. Be open to new experiences, celebrate small wins, and remind yourself that possibilities are limitless—explore every opportunity that comes your way.

> "Your task is not to seek for love, but merely to seek and find the barriers within yourself that you have built against it." -Rumi

For years, I carried the weight of trauma, unaware of its deep hold on me. But I found the strength to recognize patterns, take responsibility for my needs, and find my way back to my true self. Now, I embrace a life beyond my wildest dreams and have become the hero my younger self always needed, providing the support I once longed for.

My hope is that my story offers encouragement—a permission slip to live on your own terms. To rise above your pain, and embrace the transformative power within you. Remember, you matter, and your capacity for change is limitless. May you find the courage to honor yourself and step boldly into your redefined future. Transitioning from merely surviving to thriving is incredible. Take that step toward healing—you deserve to feel this alive, too.

Three

The Shadows We Inherit

*Transforming Generational Trauma
into Leadership Wisdom*

JENNIFER GRACE

A s I sat on my mother's paisley-patterned couch in the summer of 1992, fresh out of college, and newly turned twenty-one, I had no idea that the conversation we were about to have would set me on a path of deep introspection, healing, and ultimately, leadership. My mother's trembling lips and quivering voice hinted at the weight of the words she was about to share, words that would shatter the facade of our family history and reveal the dark shadows that had long loomed over us.

The room seemed to close in around us as my mother took a deep breath, steadying herself. I braced for impact, my mind racing through possible scenarios. Was she leaving her husband? Had someone died? Was I adopted? I glanced at my mother, seeing an older reflection of myself, and quickly dismissed the adoption theory. We were carbon copies of each other, our shared features a testament to our genetic bond. Little did I know, this resemblance would soon take on a painful new significance.

"Grandpa Don," my mother began, her voice barely above a whisper, "as you know, was very physically abusive to me as a child. But what you don't know is that from ages eight to twelves, he consistently raped me."

The world seemed to stop spinning at that moment. The sun might as well have gone black. In an instant, my perception of my family, my heritage, and myself shifted. The grandfather I had always instinctively disliked, the one I refused to hug during our visits to Milwaukee, was suddenly revealed as a monster wearing the mask of family.

As the initial shock gave way to rage, I felt a fierce, protective fury rise within me. It was a primal feeling, the kind that enables mothers to lift cars off their babies or face down armed intruders. "I'm going to fucking kill him," I spat out, my voice trembling with anger. "I'm going to Milwaukee right now, and I am going to set that motherfucker on fire."

My mother sat quietly, allowing me to vent my fury. Her silence spoke volumes—of years of pain endured, secrets kept, a strength I was only beginning to comprehend. Little did I know, this moment of raw emotion would be the first step in a long journey of healing and self-discovery, not just for me, but for both of us.

As my rage subsided, replaced by a hollow ache, memories began to surface. I remembered the summers and Christmases spent in Milwaukee, the way I would run into my grandmother Dorothy's soft arms, breathing in her freshly washed skin. And then there was Grandpa Don, towering at six-feet, three-inches, always met with my cold indifference.

"No hug for me?" he would grumble, his voice rough with cigarette smoke.

"I don't hug boys," I would reply with defiance, walking away without a care for his feelings.

My mother would trail after me, gently admonishing, "Jenny, that's not nice." But she never forced me to hug him. Now I understood why.

In the days and weeks that followed my mother's revelation, I grappled with a whirlwind of emotions. Anger, grief, confusion, and a deep sense of betrayal swirled within me. I found myself questioning everything I thought I knew about my family, about trust, about the nature of evil. How could someone do such a thing to their own child? How had my mother found the strength to survive, to raise me with love and warmth despite her trauma?

These questions would haunt me for years, shaping my worldview and, though I didn't realize it at the time, lay the groundwork for my future as a leader. They taught me early on that appearances can be deceiving, the most monstrous acts can be hidden behind a facade of normalcy, and strength often comes in forms we least expect.

It wasn't until years later, during a creative visualization exercise guided by my coach, Julia, that I would begin to truly process this trauma. As I imagined meeting my grandfather in a field, I was asked to see him not just with my eyes, but with my mind and heart. When I asked what lesson he was here to teach me, the word that fell from his lips was, "Forgiveness."

In that moment, something shifted within me. The rage that had been simmering for years began to cool, replaced by a profound understanding. Holding onto my anger and resentment was only hurting me, keeping me tethered to the past and to the very man I despised. Forgiveness, I realized, was not about excusing his actions or diminishing the pain he had caused. It was about freeing myself from the burden of hatred, about choosing to move forward unburdened by the weight of the past.

THE TURNING POINT

This realization was a turning point in my journey. It taught me a crucial lesson that would later inform my leadership style: True strength lies not in holding onto anger or seeking revenge, but in having the courage to let go, to choose healing over hatred. It's a lesson I've carried with me into every leadership role I've held, informing how I handle conflicts, how I approach difficult conversations, and how I inspire my students to overcome their own challenges.

But the shadows of my family history didn't end there. Years later, during a casual game of rummy cube with my mother on her back screened-in porch, another family secret spilled out like thick red wine onto a crisp white tablecloth.

We had been discussing her work in women's prisons, where she was helping female inmates heal from sexual abuse trauma through somatic movement and 'writing as medicine' workshops. I had made a casual remark about how I probably wouldn't last a single day in prison.

My mother's response caught me completely off guard. "Well, your Grandpa Sal lasted a year," she said, laughing it off before realizing she had revealed something I didn't know. Her hand flew to her mouth. "Oops. I thought you knew. Sorry."

I was stunned. My perfectly groomed, always impeccably dressed Italian grandfather, my father's father, a criminal? The man I remembered wearing three-piece suits with matching socks, handkerchief, and tie, adorned with solid gold cufflinks, on any given Tuesday. This couldn't be the same person.

As the story unfolded, I learned that Grandpa Sal had been a cop in Brooklyn, walking a beat that included the social clubs of infamous mobsters like Gotti and Gambino. These weren't just any restaurants; they were fronts for organized crime families. My grandfather's job, it turned out, was to keep an eye out for other cops while the mobsters counted their ill-gotten gains.

One day, the Federal Bureau of Investigation (FBI) raided one of these establishments, catching my grandfather, accepting cash in a back alley. When questioned, he refused to rat out his associates, a decision that earned him a year in prison but also the lasting loyalty of the mob.

"That's how your grandfather got his limousine business," my mother explained. "Once he was released, Gotti set him up with a fleet of limos."

Suddenly, all those childhood memories of riding in long, luxurious black cars took on a new meaning. The trips to Villa Borgesse, my grandfather's favorite Brooklyn Italian restaurant, or to Broadway shows in Manhattan—all of it funded by his loyalty to the mob.

This revelation left me conflicted. On one hand, I admired his loyalty—a trait deeply ingrained in my Brooklyn upbringing. We had been taught from a young age to always have our friends' backs, to never be a rat. It was an unspoken rule, our code of honor. On the other hand, I struggled with the knowledge that my grandfather had been on the wrong side of the law, that he had compromised his integrity as a police officer.

As I grappled with these two very different but equally shocking family histories, I began to understand that life is rarely black and white. The world is filled with shades of gray, and our ancestors–like all of us–are complex individuals shaped by their circumstances, choices, and the times they lived in.

This realization became a cornerstone of my journey towards leadership. I learned that true strength comes not from ignoring our past or pretending our families are perfect, but from confronting our history head-on and choosing how we will let it shape us. It taught me the importance of nuance in leadership, of understanding that people are multifaceted, and that even those who have made grave mistakes can possess admirable qualities.

From my mother's story, I learned the power of resilience and the importance of breaking cycles of abuse. Her courage in sharing her experience and using it to help others through her book and one-woman show, *Healing My Life: One Woman's Journey from Incest to Joy*, showed me that our deepest wounds can become sources of strength and inspiration for others.

Watching her perform her play nationwide, not just for survivors but also for young boys who had already committed sexual crimes, taught me the transformative power of vulnerability and authenticity. The way these troubled youth would open up to their clinicians after hearing my mother's story, sometimes crying and feeling empathy for the first time, drove home the point that sharing our truth can create ripples of healing far beyond ourselves.

My grandfather Sal's story, while vastly different, taught me equally valuable lessons. It showed me the complexities of loyalty and the importance of integrity. While I couldn't condone his actions, I came to understand the nuanced nature of human behavior and the power of redemption. His ability to rebuild his life after prison reminded me that it's never too late to change course and make amends.

Once brought to light, these family shadows became powerful teachers. They taught me that leadership isn't about being perfect or coming from a flawless background. Instead, it's about acknowledging our full history—the good, the bad, and the ugly—and using those experiences to cultivate empathy, understanding, and wisdom.

As a leader, I've learned to approach situations with nuance and compassion, understanding that everyone has a story and people are more than their worst mistakes or the circumstances they were born into. I've developed a keen ability to see beyond surface-level behaviors and connect with the humanity in others, even in challenging situations.

This approach has served me well in various leadership roles. When faced with my own relationship conflicts, instead of rushing to judgment, I take the time to understand the underlying factors driving each person's behavior. When making difficult decisions, I consider not just the immediate consequences, but the long-term impact on all stakeholders, always striving to act with integrity even when it's not the easiest path.

The process of healing from generational trauma has also given me invaluable tools for leadership. I've learned the importance of open communication, of creating safe spaces where difficult truths can be spoken and heard. I understand the power of vulnerability and how sharing our stories can create deep connections and inspire others to confront their own challenges.

In my leadership workshops and retreats, I often encourage participants to explore their own family histories and the unconscious patterns they might be carrying. It's amazing to see the breakthroughs that occur when people connect their current behaviors and challenges to their ancestral experiences. This work not only helps them become more self-aware leaders, but also more empathetic and understanding colleagues and mentors.

Perhaps most importantly, I've learned the transformative power of forgiveness—not just for others but for ourselves. In leadership, as in life, mistakes will be made, and difficult decisions will sometimes have unintended consequences. The ability to forgive—to let go of resentment and move forward with clear eyes and an open heart—is crucial for personal growth and effective leadership.

This lesson has been particularly valuable in high-pressure business environments where tensions can run high and conflicts can easily escalate. By modeling forgiveness and encouraging a culture where it's safe to make mistakes and learn from them, I've seen teams become more innovative, more collaborative, and ultimately more successful.

As I reflect on my family's history and my journey to leadership, I'm reminded of the words of Carl Jung: "I am not what happened to me, I am what I choose to become." The shadows of our ancestors don't have to define us. Instead, they can be the fertile soil from which we grow into stronger, wiser, more compassionate individuals and leaders.

To all those grappling with their own family histories and generational traumas, I say this: Your past does not determine your future. The sins of your fathers (or grandfathers) are not your own. You have the power to break cycles, heal, and transform your inherited shadows into beacons of light and leadership.

In embracing our full stories—the triumphs and the tragedies, the light and the dark—we become more fully human. And it is from this place of wholeness and self-acceptance that we can truly lead, inspiring others to confront their own shadows and step into their full potential.

As we journey forward, let us remember that healing is not a destination but a continual process. Leadership, too, is not a title to be achieved but a practice to be lived daily. By committing to our own healing and growth, we create ripple effects that extend far beyond ourselves, touching the lives of those we lead and creating positive change in the world.

In the end, our greatest strength as leaders comes not from pretending to be perfect, but from embracing our full humanity—shadows and all. It is in acknowledging our wounds, doing the work to heal, and choosing to lead from a place of hard-won wisdom that we truly become the leaders our world needs.

The journey of transforming generational trauma into leadership wisdom is not an easy one. It requires courage, introspection, and a willingness to face uncomfortable truths. But it is a journey worth taking, not just for our own sake, but for the sake of those we lead and the broader communities we serve.

As I continue to navigate my own path of healing and leadership, I am grateful for the lessons learned from my family's complex history. These experiences have shaped me into the leader I am today—one who leads with empathy, integrity, and a deep understanding of the human condition. They have taught me that our greatest challenges can become our greatest strengths, and by embracing our full stories, we can inspire others to do the same.

In sharing this chapter of my life, I hope to encourage other leaders to explore their own family histories, confront their inherited shadows, and use these insights as a catalyst for personal growth and more effective leadership. For it is only by understanding where we come from that we can truly chart a course for where we want to go.

Let us move forward with courage, compassion, and the knowledge that our past does not define us, but rather informs the wisdom we bring to our roles as leaders and change-makers in the world.

Four

China Dolls

A Healing Journey

MARY LEE ARANAS

I'm standing in a roomful of mirrors. My mother's reflection faces me, a twinkle in her eyes, hair soft and black, looking lovely in a magenta *qi-pao*. Behind her stands a stunning young woman in the traditional village garb of northern China, on her wedding day to my grandfather. Her chin lifts in a defiant look, fire flashes in her eyes. Behind her stands my gentle great-grandmother, worry lines on her brow. Rows of Chinese women line up like shimmering dolls in the mirrors behind them, like glimmering jewels, thousands of generations of ghosts in my mirrors.

I'm shivering, so I close my eyes, but I still feel them. Now I sense more mirrors behind me. My niece in California, professional, smart, a loving young mother. I hear her toddler son chortling with her, I feel her unborn baby snuggled within her, waiting to join our dance.

I feel behind me the presence of my New York born son, humorous, wry, thoughtful. Behind me too, I feel the presence of endless more dolls in more mirrors, great-great-grand-nephews and nieces. The whisper of a granddaughter or grandson.

My vision dispels, images turn to mist. I feel a huge tenderness for all of us. I remember what brought me to my healing and teaching path: generations of woman-wounds, sacral chakra wounds that become opportunities for growth and healing.

CYNTHIA/CHUN-HWA

My name is Yu Chun-Hwa. The year is 1943. I live in the village of Shandong in Jinan Province. I have no brothers or sisters, but I have three girl cousins from my mother's brother. I call them Big Sister, Second Sister, Third Sister. I am the youngest cousin.

We live in my grandparents' compound. My mother lives with us but my father left home five years ago when I was four, along with all the men who were not sick or elderly, with the army. Then the Japanese came. They ran up a flag in the main square. In school, we learn Japanese and speak only Japanese. In the mornings, we stand outside at assembly and sing the Japanese anthem piped over the speakers. I watch stern-faced officers wearing guns on the streets and in front of the houses as I walk home with my cousins and our *amahs*, scurrying with our faces down, trembling as we hurry home.

The relatives of our men away in the Army are called in for questioning. My mother comes home pale and shaking each time. Sometimes she is away for days. I feel sorry for her. I miss my father. Though he has been gone more than half my life, I feel I see him. I picture my *baba* walking through our door, patting my head, wrapping me in a big hug.

My mother seldom looks at me. She never touches me, except the time I spilled her face powder, and she screamed and cried, and smacked me, hard, with her hairbrush.

I guess she never wanted to be a mother. Or she's just angry and disappointed I am not a boy. Disappointed if I had to be a girl, I am not prettier, more obedient. More lovable. Instead I spend more time with her mother, my Popo. Popo makes me laugh. She tells me I'm smarter and prettier than my cousins. She saves me treats. My cousins give me the side-eye when we play in the yard, but I don't care. It makes up for my mother. I adore my Popo.

Popo says to me one night, "Sleep in my room tonight. Let your mother rest." I am happy to snuggle in with her. Mother and I share a room, and her bed when she lets me. But I have to be very still, because if I move and disturb her, she gets angry and expels me to my mat.

It gets cold in the north of China on winter nights. Popo's bed smells warm and safe. I snuggle in, sleep deeply, and dream of Father coming home.

In the morning, Mother is dead. There is blood on her pillow. I see it from around the doorway corner, peeking in, hearing hushed adult voices in the house. We hold a quiet family funeral. My family does not say much. "She had been feeling sick." I don't feel very much. Maybe stunned, relieved even. She was always cross and dissatisfied with me.

The village children whisper. "She thought she was so fancy. Too special for everyone." Some whisper she was seen out with the village men. Others say she was seen with Japanese officers. My family says nothing, but that's our way. Family matters are private.

I now live with Popo in our household of four young girls, no boys. "Four empty mouths to feed," they tease, pinching our cheeks hard enough we wince. "Four useless girls to marry out and waste all our years of feeding and housing." My cheek stings, but it's the shame and powerlessness that squat, like hungry goblins, on my chest.

In 1949, as the Japanese leave, the Communists arrive, not gently. Families with professions, education, or Army ties are all suspect. People are publicly humiliated, banished to labor camps, executed. Families divide. Some join the Party. Others are disgraced and punished.

I am a teenager now with my three girl cousins. Our relatives bundle us together, tell us to look out for each other. They give us tight squeezes. My Popo wipes her eye, looks away. I clench my jaw and lift my chin high. We join thousands of children in a mass exodus from China, following Chiang Kai-Shek's army in retreat from the People's Liberation Army. Over a million refugees flee China to crowd the two tiny islands Hainan and Taiwan (The Asianometry Newsletter). Taiwan is where we and the Nationalist government settle.

Mao declares the People's Republic of China, and the Iron Curtain closes. We will not hear any news of our families in China over the next thirty years. We girls at least, have each other. Many of the children have nobody, just a handful of teachers who fled over the waters with our schools. Penniless, I gladly sign a four-year teaching contract in exchange for free tuition at Taiwan National University. There, I meet my future husband.

Lee Chou-Hsin at nineteen is four years older than I, at fifteen. Tall, wry, stern, but his eyes twinkle. When he smiles, the corners crinkle. I call him *Lee Ge*, big brother. I feel safe with him. He disintegrates any circling boys with his icy stare. He dominates the debate team.

In music class we learn the local folk songs. There are so many mournful tunes of lovesick, homesick wanderers. His rich baritone and my clear soprano soar and dip over each other like winging swallows. I feel all soft and mushy inside.

Lee Ge had joined the Air Force at sixteen, leaving his father, mother, sisters, and younger brothers in his home village, Hangzhou. He would not see them for thirty years, some forever.

We marry after I graduate, and forge a little family in Taipei. I teach. He earns an Engineering Master's, and joins the Army. I give birth to four children. We lose our firstborn, our precious first son, a few days after his birth. A part of me is buried in Taipei forever.

We are atrocious at family planning and fertile as puppies. We terminate pregnancies we can't afford. Years later I come to regret and mourn each one of them. We toil, and money never seems enough. Fear of China's takeover looms, ever-present.

Yet I enjoy teaching. I love my work, I just somehow never feel wife enough, mother enough, woman enough. Maybe I just miss my Popo who loved me, and my baba who left me, even my Ma who didn't want me.

In 1967, we emigrate to Toronto, Canada, flying over the ocean with our three young children, hearts full of hope and not much else. None of us knows any English. We make our names easier for the Canadians: James, Cynthia, Charles, Mary, George.

Our children have an easier time learning the language than we do, but they still get bullied at school, as I get taunted crossing the street, and my husband gets called "boy" by the neighbor.

Our children grow up sounding like Canadians. I work my way to become a published Associate Professor at the University of Toronto. James has to repeat his Master's in this country, but eventually he becomes a civil engineer for the City of Nepean in Ottawa.

For eight years, I commute weekends on an eight-hour bus ride between Ottawa and Toronto, so we can both work, and maintain our family.

I am in Toronto when I hear my husband has had open-chest surgery in an Ottawa hospital.

MARY I-CHUN LEE ARANAS

My father, James Chou-Hsin Lee, fell ill in my twentieth summer. One day in our suburban Ottawa house, my fit, healthy dad felt short of breath, and visited the hospital. A cancerous thymoma covered his chest. They operated all day into night. The mass engulfed his ribs and organs. He needed chemotherapy and radiotherapy the remaining five years of his life. He was fifty-five when he passed.

I dated older men in those years: my professor, my boss, my director. I was twenty-four when I married, a year before Dad passed. He blessed us, in his raspy voice: "Take care of each other." We are taking care of each other still, four decades later.

In Spring 2001, my son is nearly six. We live in New York, and I am visiting my mother in Toronto. Mummy's hair grew back during her glorious brief remission. It is short, lush, and wavy, like soft-serve vanilla ice cream. I could swear it sparkles with icing sugar. My brothers and I gaze in awe. She is a radiant, smiling, snow-haired princess.

Widowed at fifty, Mummy remarried a Chinese widower Daddy's same age. But now at sixty-seven, she has breast cancer. We caress her cheek. She purrs, eyes fluttering. By November she will leave us to join Daddy. But now I gently brush her hair, and it brings up a memory for me.

It's 1965 in Taipei, I'm crying in my stiff school uniform. The amah brushes my hair into tight pigtails. "No! I want Ma to do it!" I swat her hand, tears exploding.

"Ai-ya! What can I do! Tai-Tai, she wants you!" The teenage girl exclaims.

Ma is packing her bicycle to go teach foreigners Chinese. "*Tao yan!* So much trouble! Ma has to work!" And off she goes, pedaling fast, my strong, smart, beautiful mother, raising three small kids in a tiny flat, baba away in the Army.

In November 2001, Mummy left us to join our dad. She was sixty-seven. He'd left us at fifty-five, so he'd been waiting a while for her. I imagined them singing together, their voices dovetailing, turning the lonely wanderers' songs into joyful homecoming love songs.

For me, living in New York, Mummy's death coming two months after September 11 felt extra devastating. It also brought a new, crystal clarity that would change my life path. This was my new clarity: both my parents died of cancers on their heart and chest. When they fell ill, he was a vigorous fifty, she, an active sixty-five. Both were child refugees, war orphans of two violent wars. And both carried emotional wounds they never once discussed, expressed, or released.

Their turmoil passes to us, their children, and through us to our children, the next generation. I felt it in my childhood, teens, and adult life. My crystal-clear conviction that my parents' wounds were weights they never released led me to choose a healing path for myself and my world.

If Daddy's death spurred me to marry a New York actor/director/musician and "run away" from Canada to be an actress for twenty years, Mummy's death transformed me into a healer. I was certified in 2001 as a yoga teacher, and have been full-time teaching, healing, and mentoring, ever since.

Every healing path I'm on continues to teach and nourish me, and help me nourish others. I love discovering the strengths and synchronicities in them. Yoga, Acro Yoga, Reiki, Non-Violent Communication, Thai Bodywork, Yoga Nidra Meditation, Healing Prayer, Writing, Breathwork, Woman-Centered Coaching.

MOTHER MARY

I stand again in the room of mirrors. They see me now, they see each other. Grandma has a tear in her eye as she reaches for my mother. Great-grandma winks at me. Behind me I can sense my niece's tender smile. She holds her two babies and stands in her own room of mirrors, her mother before her, and behind her the grandchildren yet to be. She nods at my son who shimmers behind me. My silver mirrors don't yet show those behind him, but I feel them.

We are owning the sacredness of our bodies, with our feelings, senses, emotions, desires, our "feeling-place" of who we are. I relax my breath and let them breathe through me. I feel these women forgiving themselves and each other. I feel them embracing themselves and each other.

With pleasure I see my other children, multitudes of men and women in my halls of mirrors: my yogi daughters and sons, my soul children and grandchildren. I see those I've coached, mentored, taught, guided, or healed—and those they've coached, mentored, taught, guided, and healed.

My teachers share the space with my grandmothers, beaming in this room where they meet and extend their crystalline light through me to the world. I close my eyes, and lift my hands. "I am a reflection of all the light that shines through me," someone says.

A ringing of voices. All the dolls are singing and swaying. We are moving, dancing together. Free, loved, and loving.

Five

Embracing the Journey

From Scars to Strength

FALON BIRTH

"**S**peed humps ahead," states a sign hanging in a friend's garage. The bold black letters on the bright yellow background caught my eye and made me pause. Staring at it, I thought, We all need a not-so-subtle reminder like this in our lives. How many times could I have used this nudge, reminding me that life isn't just a smooth ride to all the goodies?

I am the eldest of five children. My parents, who shared a birthday and had known each other since grade school, divorced shortly after my first sister was born. Despite my mother's best efforts, we struggled and moved often. In those early years, I was haunted by feelings I had no words for at that early age. Looking back, I now recognize those feelings as displacement and a fear of not belonging, planting the seeds of my lifelong search for a place to fit in.

When my sister and I were just two and four years old, Carl, our first stepfather, entered our lives. He had a beautiful, wide smile that reached the corners of his blue eyes. At first, his gentle demeanor made me feel safe and loved. However, Carl soon became my first lesson in the ways people can deceive and mislead. While he was tender and affectionate with my baby sister, he made it painfully clear that she was the cuter, more lovable child. Even at that tender age, I learned to hide my feelings of rejection and sadness, knowing that showing my emotions would only highlight what I believed were my glaring shortcomings. Worst yet, this would also mark the beginning of sexual, physical, and verbal abuse by another family member.

The first time I experienced the abuse, I was consumed by a fear so intense and violating that it felt like being thrown out of a five-story window with nothing to hold. Frozen in place, I experienced searing lightning bolts clashing in my head as my young mind struggled to comprehend the situation. My only defense was to clench my teeth and squeeze my eyes shut. I wanted to move, but my arms and legs felt like weights, and every finger and toe tingled with pins and needles. My chest felt so heavy, my throat shrunken. I thought, Surely this means I am going to die.

But I did not die that night or any other that my attacker would visit. I would, however, fear sleeping long after the abuse ended.

As the oldest, I was the protector, leader, and trailblazer of my family. The responsibility to be perfect weighed heavily on me—I had to set good examples for my siblings, leaving little to no room for error. This immense pressure turned into an insatiable need for control over our circumstances. I strived for perfection at home, school, and work, becoming the pillar of all things good for my family.

To ensure others were comfortable, I learned to make myself very small, sacrificing my own happiness for the sake of others. Missing deep and meaningful connections, I struggled under the relentless pressure of perfection. I buried my self-doubt, fear, and feelings of scarcity, constantly fighting the urge to run and hide. I have always been empathetic and sensitive to others' feelings, often at the expense of my own well-being. It felt selfish to meet my own needs when so many people had real problems. This, I now realize, was my ego driving my life—if I was the one giving help, then I did not have to admit that I needed it, too.

By the time I turned eighteen, I had already been living on my own for two years. I bought a small home with my then-boyfriend. A year later we married, and by the time I was twenty-three, we had two beautiful daughters. Despite our growing family, the relationship was draining. My husband, who also came from a difficult background, offered little in terms of love and support. I often felt alone, haunted by the constant fear that he would give up and leave. Sleep deprived, I dragged myself to my teaching job, which I took to fund my degree in child development, convincing myself that I could love and grow enough for both of us.

Then, without warning, my world was turned upside down. My husband, my partner of over ten years, was having an affair. Just like that, I received an emotional eviction notice from the life I knew. Fear gripped me.

How would I secure health insurance? How would I guide my kids through this pain? How could I manage the mortgage on my own?

These debilitating questions hit me like waves crashing against rocks. I felt ungrounded with nothing to hold onto and no respite from the pain. This experience was bigger than anything I had ever faced, transforming me on a molecular level.

WALKING THROUGH THE FEAR

In retrospect, this life-altering period was exactly what I needed to uncover my inner strength. After months of therapy, uncovering more affairs, and separating from him, I was ready to move forward. I put my house up for sale and secured an apartment for my girls and me.

To anyone going through a similar experience, I want to say this: I was terrified throughout this entire process. By walking through that fear, I learned bravery. Each small victory gave me the confidence to take the next brave step, and then another. Looking back, I realize this journey helped me discover the badass within me.

Every day, I started writing a list of things I was proud of, from big accomplishments to small victories. I began to see how even the little things were steppingstones to my goals. All I needed was to free myself from the confines of my mind.

This newfound recognition sparked curiosity within me. What else could I achieve if I dared to be brave? This marked one of many rebirths in my life. I loved the work I was doing, and life looked brighter. I was not just living it; I was embodying it in my walk, talk, and smile. I felt good! For the first time, I saw my value and understood what I meant to my children, family, and friends. I realized how important I was in their lives and what I contributed.

As a busy single mom, I began to see my two-hour drive to work not as a hassle but as precious me-time. I played uplifting music and listened to motivational speakers like Wayne Dyer, Louise Hay, and Brené Brown. Throughout my life, I had been collecting a proverbial sack filled with tricks and strategies for handling uncomfortable situations. These were my tools—some healthy, others destructive coping mechanisms developed over time to survive. Listening to daily motivational talks became one of my favorite tools, elevating me for the daily turbulence of life.

I began to ask myself some tough questions. What are the best solutions for me? What supports my ultimate purpose?

REUNITED WITH MY PASSION FOR LIFE

I was taking command of my present and future, doing what was best for me, regardless of what others thought. I created an inner sanctuary where I could retreat. In this space, I felt free, letting my mind wander and indulging in my imagination. Here, I found passion and hunger for my life.

When spiraling thoughts threatened to overwhelm me, I played the gratitude game. I looked around and started giving thanks for ordinary things. It might be as simple as appreciating my washing machine because I did not have to wash clothes by hand or my soft bed, which allowed me to get a good night's rest. This practice was not a one-time fix but a lifelong journey of building a life rooted in gratitude and finding new ways to express it.

The intuition I had tried so hard to silence over the years was returning to guide me. At first, this loud inner voice frightened me. Was I losing my mind? Was this healthy? Yet, this inner voice, once hushed, grew louder each day, demanding my attention. I had no choice but to listen if I wanted to advance toward my dreams with confidence.

Silencing my perfectionism often sent me into a whirlwind of emotions. The path was there; I just needed to break through the barriers and clear the way. For the first time, I gave myself permission to feel. I laughed and smiled whenever I could, not because everything was easy, but because I wanted to show gratitude. No matter how many difficult encounters I faced, I knew I would conquer them. My present and future were completely in my hands.

I no longer fear my big feelings, big heart, big mind, and big ideas. Instead, I listen for that gentle nudge from within, signaling its time. I believe in the power of self-talk. When I struggle, I remind myself with love and compassion that I am strong in the face of adversity. I have all the tools necessary to stand up for myself and others. Despite relentless opposition, I have faith in my ability to do the right thing.

I do not carry anger from my past. My past helped shape who I am today, and for that, I am grateful. Over the years since my divorce and numerous other trials, I now see the world and all my experiences as teaching moments. When I meet someone new, I think about what they will teach me, focusing less on what I get and more on what I contribute.

I also pay close attention to my needs and ensure they are met, allowing me to show up as my best self in all that I do. Living in your truth encourages others to embrace their own power, even if you are unaware of it. I hold space for myself, using my unique journey to gain insight and wisdom, which helps me make a difference in the lives of those around me. Confidence in myself allows me to extend myself to others in meaningful ways.

Making peace with your past creates space for new people and experiences. I am now married to the love of my life, and we share four beautiful children. My relationships now reflect everything that provides meaning to me. Through self-realization, we can achieve the success we deserve in our struggles. I no longer need to compromise my beliefs. I live by my values and remain true to my path by staying connected to what is in my heart. My life transformed in ways I had never imagined. Each day was an opportunity to grow, learn, and embrace the fullness of my being. As I continued cultivating my inner sanctuary, I blossomed into the person I was always meant to be.

One pivotal moment came when I decided to pursue a long-held dream of mine: writing. Ideas had been simmering in my mind for years, but it was not until I embraced my inner strength and self-worth that I found the courage to bring it to life.

My family continues to serve as a central source of joy and inspiration. My children thrive in their pursuits, each finding their own passions and paths. My husband and I grow closer, our bonds strengthening with each shared experience and challenge. We made it a point to cultivate a home environment filled with love, laughter, and open communication. While sitting around the dinner table with my family, I reflect on how far we have come. The laughter of my children, the warmth of my husband's hand in mine, and the feeling of togetherness brought tears of gratitude to my eyes. We have faced many trials, but we have come out stronger, more resilient, and more connected than ever.

Throughout my life, I met countless individuals who inspired me with their own stories of courage and perseverance. Each person I encountered reaffirmed my belief in the power of the human spirit. I saw firsthand how a supportive community could lift someone up, providing the strength they needed to overcome their struggles.

As I continued to grow in my personal and professional life, I remained committed to my own self-care and development. I never lost sight of the importance of nurturing my inner world, knowing it was the foundation upon which everything else was built. I continued my practices of gratitude, self-reflection, and mindful living, always striving to be the best version of myself.

Looking back on my journey, I realized that every hardship, every moment of doubt, and every painful experience had been a stepping stone to this beautiful life. I learned to embrace my imperfections, see my scars as symbols of strength, and use my experiences to uplift others.

Today, I stand as a testament to the power of resilience and the transformative potential of self-love and acceptance. My life is a tapestry woven with threads of hope, courage, and unwavering faith. As I move forward, I do so with an open heart, ready to face whatever comes my way with grace and determination.

To anyone reading this, know that you too have the power to transform your life. Embrace your journey, with all its twists and turns and speed bumps, and trust you are exactly where you need to be.

Six

From Doubt to Destiny

What If You Fly?

COTY WALKER

One sleepless night, I was plagued by a pesky voice in my head repeating, *What if I fail?*

I tossed and turned, unable to sleep, my mind racing with the repeated thought of failure. Around 4 a.m., I dozed off for about half an hour. Suddenly, a stronger, more empowered voice awoke me that softly countered, *Oh my darling, but what if you fly?*

The next day, exhausted yet resolute, I realized I could no longer silence that voice. I had to make a change.

For more than ten years, I had been at a crossroads, always choosing the easy path lured by the safe and secure financial reward despite the lack of fulfillment it brought me. I had worked for big multinationals in Europe, advancing positions due to a few strategic moves. However, I kept ignoring the persistent feeling I was meant to do something different with my life.

High stress levels, unhappiness, and the hope that my next job opportunity would bring fulfillment were constant themes in my life. I often thought about reinventing myself and living a life of purpose, but I constantly asked myself: *What is my purpose? How does one find their purpose?*

Towards the end of 2018, I had been living in Canada for five years and reached the peak of my unhappiness at a job in a small company. Within a few years, I rose to the top, but my stress levels kept increasing during the three years I worked there. I hadn't realized it was taking a toll on my family life. Trying to juggle a high-stress job with two pre-teen boys with Attention Deficit Hyperactivity Disorder (ADHD) and their extracurricular activities overwhelmed me.

Evenings at home, trying to get dinner ready in time to take the kids to hockey or other activities, became a second full-time job for my husband and I. We divided activities and conquered what we could. More than once, I showed up to a game or practice with either the wrong kid or the right kid with the wrong equipment.

One evening, after a hard day at work, I was trying to get dinner ready in time and keep the times, arenas, and kids sorted out in my mind so I wouldn't make any mistakes. My youngest son, Kyle, eight years old at the time, came to me with a sparkle in his eye to talk about something. It was more than my tired and overstimulated brain could handle at that moment, and I snapped at him as he broke my concentration.

All I remember was the look of surprise and hurt on his face as he said, "Mom, I can't talk to you anymore. You are always in a bad mood." Then he walked away.

My heart broke into a million pieces as I realized that I had become the type of parent I didn't want to be.

At that moment, my husband, Wade, who was helping organize our chaotic evening, looked at me with compassion and said, "Hon, Kyle is right, something needs to change."

I knew my husband was right, and I knew my son was right. But if I only knew what needed to change or where to start, everything would be alright. Again, the little voice in my head wondered, *What is my purpose?*

SYNCHRONICITY

I believe in synchronicity and in the perfect timing from the Universe. As 2019 progressed, we confronted something unprecedented that forced the world to slow down. The COVID-19 pandemic changed everything. The company I worked for started losing clients at a rapid rate; my stress and my workload increased; and soon enough I found myself out of a job. At the same time, other businesses created more online options, and suddenly a huge number of resources were at my fingertips. There were more webinars about finding purpose that I could keep up with! I followed every single methodology out there, becoming a serial webinar attendee in my quest to find my path.

Wade and I decided that I would give myself some time to find my path. I figured I would have it down in three months, from September to December, and by the beginning of the following year, I would have more clarity on what I was doing with my career and the rest of my life.

January 2020 rolled around, and I realized that I didn't have an answer. Regardless, I updated my resume, feeling pressured to contribute financially, and sent a few applications to get interviews. After every interview, I would have a quick debrief with my husband, and I surprised myself by talking about every opportunity with negativity. After a few conversations, it became evident I needed more time to figure things out and going back to corporate life might not be the right thing for me. It was time to reinvent myself. This realization brought me back to square one. I felt lost and scared.

I signed up for more webinars, widening my search; I was open to anything and everything. I learned so many things and was inspired by so many people! I had always been a lifelong learner, and this was right up my alley.

I also started investing in my health. With the work pressure off my shoulders, I invested time in healthier meals for me and my family and started an amazing fitness routine. It was time to take care of my body, and the results started to show. I loved the results, and I started to love myself again.

Wade and I began hiking more often and spending more time outdoors. The pandemic brought socialization restrictions, and as we are blessed to live only one hour away from the magnificent Rocky Mountains, we spent plenty of time in nature.

As the pandemic's restrictions started to relax, I started socializing again outdoors, and one of my favorite activities became walks with friends.

THE WALK THAT CHANGED THE COURSE OF MY LIFE

I started walking with my neighbour and friend, Lisa, an amazing human and executive coach. She had been following my career dilemma, and during one of our walks, she asked insightful questions about what I wanted to do with my life. Her questions brought clarity to my thought process, made me evaluate my options and motivations, and I realized things were becoming more clear.

In that moment, I made the commitment to overcome my fears to create the life I wanted for myself. It was the first time in more than fifteen years that I felt excited about my future! I decided to become a life coach with a focus on health and wellness. Wouldn't it be wonderful to help people find their path and their purpose? There must be others questioning their choices, needing to align careers with their purpose, or going through various transitions, right?

I went home after my walk, excited and a bit terrified. My head was spinning, and my heart was full.

Would I have the courage to make the change? What would Wade, my biggest ally, think? Would I have his support? What would my friends and family think? What would all my professional connections on social media think?

I needed to take some time to reflect. I didn't want to talk to anyone just yet.

Awakening – What If I Fly?

For the next few days and nights, I tried not to dwell on the thought, but it lingered in the back of my mind, simmering like a winter stew. I avoided these thoughts at night until a couple of nights later, I found myself unable to sleep, with the phrase, *What if you fail?* repeatedly echoing in my mind.

One of my favorite poems is "What If You Fail?" by Eric Hansen. This line from his poem kept coming back to me: "What if you fail?" Yes, I was afraid of failure. *What if I fail?*

Finally, I fell into a restless sleep around 4 a.m. About thirty minutes later, a strong, empowered voice came to me and decisively but gently said, *Oh my darling, but what if you fly?*, another line from the poem.

Our alarm went off at 7 a.m. as usual, but I asked Wade to please take care of breakfast for the kids since I had a sleepless night. I made it out of bed at 10 a.m. and found my husband in the kitchen making himself a cup of tea between meetings.

He looked at me and said, "Rough night, honey?"

I looked at him and told him about my walk with Lisa a few days ago, my decision to become a health and life coach, and about the poem and the voices in my head all night.

I stood there terrified about his reaction. As I mentioned, he is my biggest ally and best friend, and it was important to have his support. He took a minute to process what I said, gave me a loving look, and said, "What If You Fly Coaching. That is a brilliant name for your business. After my meeting, I can help you see if the domain name is available for your website."

With that, he gave me a quick kiss and went back to his office for his next meeting.

My heart was full. The only way to describe the next year of my life is by using the word bliss.

It was a complete honeymoon as I immersed myself in the world of coaching, took many wonderful courses, met incredible people, and grew and healed as a person. Most importantly, I found my purpose, which is to help people during periods of life transitions. I became a health and life coach, learning that beliefs create thoughts, thoughts create feelings, feelings create behaviours/habits, and behaviours/habits create results.

Therefore, I now invest in my overall health—physical, mental, and spiritual—as I firmly believe that health is the doorway to transformation and the first step in creating the life I want.

I established many different new practices for myself and tried various tools. Some worked better than others; some stuck, some didn't. One of the practices that became a regular part of my routine is my ten minutes of daily meditation.

Having a brain that stays in race mode makes it difficult for me to meditate. Even though I started with just three minutes, it felt almost impossible to get through it. Mantras didn't really work for me either. What worked was counting to twenty-five and making every number a breath. This, coupled with a beautiful mala bead rosary that I acquired, provided the needed stimulation and calming effect I needed for my busy brain and soul to recharge. Every time I make it to twenty-five, I start again from one. The mala beads help me pace myself and provide tactile feedback, helping me realize if I am rushing my breathing.

I loved this one-hundred-and-eight mala bead rosary so much I bought a smaller one that I use for affirmations. Now I dedicate an extra couple of minutes at the end of my meditation to say five or six positive affirmations aloud as many times as there are beads. I change these affirmations occasionally, when I feel that something has changed in my life, such as when one of my affirmations has already manifested or if I feel it's not relevant anymore. This small twenty-seven mala bead bracelet has become my favorite ritual.

THE JOURNEY FROM DOUBT TO FLIGHT

I embraced the concept of "What If You Fly?" and transformed my life, finding fulfillment and purpose through my journey. Each step, from the sleepless night filled with doubts to the awakening moment that sparked change, has taught me the power of believing in myself.

By confronting my fears and making the decision to pursue a path aligned with my passions, I not only reshaped my career but also my entire outlook on life. My dedication to health, wellness, and continuous learning has not only benefited me but also those around me.

As a health and life coach, I now guide others through their own transformations, helping them discover their true potential and the joy that comes from living a purposeful life. The journey from doubt to flight has been an extraordinary adventure, one I am committed to sharing with others so they, too, can spread their wings and soar.

Seven

Beyond Guilt and Shame

A Mother's Journey to Forgiveness

ANGELA ZALMAN-MOONEY

I walked out of my son's bedroom, his screams and heart-wrenching cries trailing off into the distance. Just moments before I was standing over his small body as he cowarded in front of me full of fear, and I was full of rage threatening to spank him for something my mind no longer remembers. I saw the sheer terror in his beautiful blue eyes, and that look invoked the feeling I had as a child: The person who was supposed to love him most was terrifying.

I collapsed into a chair at the dining room table, my head heavy in my hands, tears streaming down my face. I couldn't keep living like this. Every fiber of my being screamed for escape. This is what my life has become. We've been doing this toxic dance for two years now. The visions I held of being a kind and compassionate mom were a shattered dream. I was just surviving at this point. The childhood I swore I would never live again was replaying, but this time, I was the mother inflicting trauma on my child. I blamed our son for the chaos in our life. I blamed him for the person he triggered inside of me. I was soaked in so much shame. I knew what was happening in our relationship was not good for any of us, but I didn't know how to escape it.

What was wrong with me?

I walked upstairs to my husband's home office, my posture slumped in defeat.

"Eric, I can't live like this anymore. This is not the life I signed up for." I trembled, my voice cracked. "I have to leave."

I remembered the promise I made to myself after leaving an abusive relationship twelve years earlier: I wouldn't be miserable for anyone, not even my son.

Eric, tears welling up in his eyes, reached for me with shaking arms. He could tell I was serious. Every time I sought refuge he knew I inched closer and closer to my breaking point.

"I can't do this life without you," he pleaded, his voice raw, but I could offer no answers.

We clung to each other, seeped in the depths of our guilt, shame, and the realization that something had to change. We'd tried every therapy, read every parenting book, taken all the classes—none of the techniques worked. They only seemed to make things worse. Our child had such big emotional outbursts, and I was at a loss on how to help him process them.

Emotions were hard for me. Growing up, my mom had big feelings, so there was never any space for mine. I learned to turn my empathy off. It was weird. When big emotions entered the room, it was like a switch inside of me went off, *nope I can't deal with that today,* and I'd go into problem-solving mode. Except I couldn't figure out how to solve this problem, so I'd convinced myself he'd be better off without me.

I thought for sure when I had my own child that the switch would stay on. Not only did he come from my body, but we tried for years to have him. I didn't understand him, and the small connection we had continued to dwindle, and I knew he felt the disconnect and the misunderstanding. Eric didn't seem to have the same troubles connecting with him. Clearly, I was the problem. I'd struggled from the beginning to attach to him. Nurturing wasn't natural, and everyone around me seemed to have this beautiful gift of love and connection to their child. Every time I tried to relate to him, I felt like a complete fraud.

I am a woman, and that's what we are genetically designed to do, nurture, but I didn't feel nurturing. I loved him with every cell in my body, but I didn't like the person I became around him, the yelling, the constant fighting, the shame, the guilt. He triggered parts of myself I didn't know existed. If things continued, I'd only resent him; I already hated myself. What was wrong with me? Was I broken?

Memories flooded back of the drive home from the hospital after my son's birth, leaving him in the neonatal intensive care unit for what felt like eternity. I felt so dark, so empty. I couldn't imagine how any mother could leave their child behind the way my birth mother abandoned me as a small, helpless infant. Yet here I was ready to leave my family. I thought to myself, *This is how mothers do it.* It made sense to me now. That was the last time I remembered feeling like a real mother.

It had been a year since I confessed to my husband my overwhelming desire to leave our family and start anew. I promised him I'd try for a little longer, but every day felt like a struggle. I dragged myself out of bed, barely keeping up appearances while my husband took on the bulk of the parenting. My son began showing signs of severe anxiety—chewing on his shirt, having panic attacks when voices were raised, and emotional outbursts at school. Up until this point, his emotional dysregulation was isolated to inside our home. I knew deep down that I was the cause; that my unresolved trauma and inability to self-regulate was hurting my child. The shame and guilt consumed me. I couldn't change the past, but I couldn't figure out how to give myself the grace I needed to move forward.

A BEACON OF HOPE

I sought help through therapy, spiritual workshops, reading, podcasts, journaling, and meditation. These tools brought awareness to my patterns, but I kept circling back to shame and guilt. It felt like I would take two steps forward and four steps back. The loop felt neverending. That's when I met Sonia, my future mentor.

She was a vibrant woman with a commanding presence and unapologetic confidence. I admired her vulnerability and how she navigated her own trauma using tarot and human design. I entered our mentorship wanting to learn more about human design because I had taken a human design course that opened my eyes to a whole other understanding of myself and my family, and I wanted to work one-on-one with someone to dig deeper. I also hoped she'd have an easy fix for my problems. I wished she'd pull some tarot cards and tell me that a spiritual retreat with a shaman would solve everything. But surprise, life doesn't work that way!

The more Sonia and I worked together, the more she emphasized a practice of curiosity, non-judgment, and unconditional love. I understood curiosity, and I wondered why people made the choices they did. But what did non-judgment and unconditional love look like in practice? We live in a world of judgment and conditional love. How could I tell if I was thriving without comparison?

Comparison and judgment are so ingrained in us. I thought of myself as pretty non-judgmental, yet I was struggling with not passing judgment and loving myself unconditionally. When you start to break down your life with these three principals, you start to realize just how judgmental and conditional your love really is.

I recalled an entry entitled "Hypocrisy" from the *Tao of Motherhood*, a book gifted to me by my mother-in-law that read, "When you forget that you and your children are instruments of the One, dogma takes over. When truth is forgotten, acceptance, tolerance, compassion, and flexibility give way to judgment, intolerance, meanness and rigidity. Hypocrisy follows."

I had to let go of judgment and comparison, which filled me with guilt and shame, in order to truly heal. I started reading *Letting Go* by Dr. David Hawkins, and he talks about shame and guilt being of the lowest frequency, and how the only way in letting go and releasing an emotion is to surrender and move through it. He discusses moving through the feeling and not the thoughts because our thoughts are self-reinforcing and never ending.

I started to become curious when I would react to my son's behavior. *Why is this triggering me?* I knew from all the classes I attended, the books I read, and the podcasts I listened to that the consensus was that the parent needs to change in order to create the most effective change in their child. This was my motivator. I wanted a different life for my child than I had, so it had to start with me.

For months, I'd been practicing this approach, and I hadn't been able to put my finger on the true reason for the triggers until one day it hit me. I have spent my entire parenting journey determined not to be the same as my mother and trying to control everything. I became conscious of a painful pattern: My mom shamed me for not meeting her expectations, and I shamed my son for not being the perfect child, and the cycle went on. I felt like as a mother, I was held to a higher standard, and because I couldn't forgive my mom for her mistakes then I wasn't allowed to forgive myself for mine. How could I possibly learn my lesson if I granted myself grace?

CREATING A NEW RHYTHM

During this time, I became a certified hypnotherapist. I'd spent my entire life facing my shadows, so I thought learning hypnosis to help others was an obvious next step. I started working with a client on her triggers in hypnosis sessions when I realized I needed to take my own practice deeper. Now that I was conscious and aware of the true root cause of my reactivity, it was time to deep dive into my subconscious to reprogram that part of me.

One evening I drew a warm bath, my sanctuary since childhood. The soft glow of candles, the soothing scent of lavender, and the gentle fizz of healing salt set the tone. As I sank into the water, I took five deep breaths, letting myself relax, and whispered, "I surrender to this moment."

I called in my guides, angels, goddesses, and ancestors, asking for the healing I needed. With each breath my body relaxed. Most times I struggle getting out of my head, so I always start meditation or hypnosis with the song "I Release Control" by Alexa Sunshine Rose. Once I noticed my mind quiet and my body relaxed, I put on my recorded self-hypnosis. As the words began to rhythmically seduce me, I began replaying the parenting moments I felt deepest shame and guilt about, especially the day I wanted to leave my family.

For years, I'd sat in that self-judgment, adding to it daily. Now, in this peaceful state, I let the memories surface without judgment or self-criticism. I breathed through the discomfort, repeating internally, *I surrender to this moment with curiosity, non-judgment, and unconditional love.*

As memories flowed in, scenes from my childhood appeared, but this time, I saw them through my mother's eyes. I'd spent years holding her accountable for her mistakes, but now I saw her pain, her unfulfilled dreams. I saw a woman overwhelmed by responsibilities she never asked for, just trying to survive. I saw the parallels between our lives, the unmet expectations, the guilt, and the shame. I allowed myself to take a bird's-eye view of my life, and the animosity I held for years began to lift. A wave of forgiveness washed over me, and as I opened my eyes, tears streaming down my face, I forgave my mom. In forgiving her, I found space to forgive myself. The weight of shame for not being the perfect mom lifted, and I felt gratitude for recognizing there's always room to grow, to become a better mother. Releasing the shame and guilt that had defined me for so long allowed me to be more present for my son.

Letting go of the shame and guilt tied to past memories granted me true control over my life. For years, shame and self-judgment kept me anchored in regrets or consumed by future worries. But I've come to realize I can't alter the past, and the future remains a mystery. Releasing this burden has allowed me to fully embrace the present moment.

A quote from Richard Rudd's book, *Gene Keys*, resonates deeply with me, especially as it relates to my Core Wound in Gene Keys. "As parents heal their own emotional issues and raise the frequency of their DNA, they pass on healthy emotional patterns to their children, who then continue this legacy. There is no role of greater importance or service to humanity than that of being a parent."

This rings painfully true. I spent years drowning in shame, feeling unworthy to be my son's mother, and in doing so, I missed precious moments of his early life. But as I've worked through that shame and guilt, I've transformed into a calmer, more present mother. My son's anxiety has diminished, our bond has never been stronger, and I've become the nurturing mother I always aspired to be. The power of inner healing is profound, and it creates ripples that touch generations.

When you're ready to release your own guilt and shame, start by getting curious and asking yourself why? Then find your safe space, be it a cozy chair, a peaceful spot in nature, or even your bathroom. Put in earbuds with calming sounds and focus on your breath, giving yourself permission to surrender.

If you think, "My mind is too restless," just try. Create a space for your subconscious to emerge and guide you. It wants to heal you. Just bring curiosity, non-judgment, and unconditional love.

Eight

❦

Gaining Life from Loss

Creating a Living Journal to
Visualize Your Growth

DELAYNA ANDERSON

Having life and living sound similar side by side, but my mind comprehends two totally different concepts. To have life means having the biological functions to exist; while living means to have the wonder, awe, and appreciation of being alive. I used to live, enjoying what and who I had, surrounding myself with happiness and love. That is until my son, a precious and loving soul, no longer had life.

When you have children, you don't expect to lose them. As a parent, you inadvertently plan their lives from infancy to adulthood. The anticipation of their first word, graduation, and wedding day grows over the years as they reach new milestones.

I was a single mother of two, a boy and a girl. My son was the youngest and spoiled. His sister insists that I started him late with everything. Such as having to do chores around the house or making his own food because he was my favorite. They were always told that they were both my favorite. She, my favorite daughter and he, my favorite son. The three of us spent time together as well as individually doing our favorite things. I watched horror movies with her and played video games with him.

With a two-year age gap, the personalities of my children were different. They bickered the way children do, but the love between them was immense. She was always firm with her younger brother but also acted as a caregiver and teacher to him. They shared a secret handshake and even made-up words only they understood. Those were the moments that eased my mind as they got older because I knew when I was no longer here, they would always have each other. Little did I know, the certainty I felt with that notion would shatter one day.

He was fourteen when he passed away; it was sudden and unexpected. The most difficult thing I have ever experienced. That day will forever be etched in my brain, and it triggered the worst bout of depression I have endured.

DISBELIEF AND GRIEF

It was mid-December 2021, and the days leading up to and after his death are both vivid and blurred. On that Monday, I was looking forward to finishing up my Christmas shopping and spending the weekend with the kids for my birthday. I couldn't help but feel that this year was ending on a great note. I had liberated myself from working a job that no longer made me happy, a relationship that was abusive, and now I had more time to dedicate to my family and self. I felt determined to make this the Christmas that I would give my children the absolute best. So, I spent the day shopping for their respective lists and decorations we would put up together.

Prior to that year, I was always nervous around Christmas. The kids would give me their wish list, and I could maybe afford one or two things on them. They were always grateful for their gifts, but I never felt like it was enough. However, this was the year that I felt confident in my holiday cheer. It was the purest feeling of happiness I'd felt in a long time.

After getting home, I planned out the rest of my week. I would work Tuesday and Wednesday, wrap gifts on Thursday, and on Friday pick up the kids from school early, play board games, put up the Christmas tree, and eat pizza. That is the timeline I long to live in, but the Universe had something different in store.

On Tuesday, I received a video call from my son while I was at work. His appearance didn't look good and he told me as much. At first, it didn't seem like anything to alarm me. Since he was staying with my parents, I asked him to call them to let them know so they could help him feel some relief. However, he called me back a few moments later with my father by his side saying that he needed me. There was never a second thought of whether I should leave work or not because my son was never one to complain about not feeling good.

As I was walking to the house, my mother was walking my son out. He was in shorts and a T-shirt with my father's oversized coat draped onto his shoulders. The sight of him filled me with worry, and we were off to the nearest emergency facility. Throughout the night there were feelings of angst and calm. There were questions, tests, doctors, and nurses in and out. No one had answers; therefore, a transfer of facilities was necessary. However, there would never be any answers for what afflicted my son that night. The morning of December 15, 2021, my affectionate, generous, and fun-loving baby boy was gone.

The months following my son's passing, I didn't work. I didn't see family or friends, and I even became somewhat of an absent parent in my daughter's life. I was no longer interested in celebrating my birthday or Christmas. The pain, anger, and guilt I felt from that day forward was immeasurable. There were times when the visions and sounds of the hours before his death would replay in my mind with the clarity of the day it happened.

I began to lose hope for my future and couldn't fathom how I could ever move on without him. Little things triggered me, seeing or hearing anything that sparked memories of him. It became difficult to try or do things he once enjoyed or would have enjoyed. Grapes made me cry. It was one of the things he asked to have for breakfast shortly before leaving this world.

It had been almost a month by the time we were able to lay him to rest. I remember very little from that day. The best memory has to offer is kissing my baby for the last time, covering him with the liner and closing the lid to his casket. I couldn't bring myself to cry as I watched my family, his friends, and school staff come into the church with looks of disbelief and sadness upon their faces. There was this emotion within me that said I had to be strong for everyone else who also felt the misery of our situation. There was a connection he had with each of those individuals, so it became their loss as well.

I became less aware of what was going on around me with each passing day. As the holiday's rolled around into the new year, I knew my behavior became more avoidant. As his birthday approached, I wanted to cancel all the plans I had because I wasn't ready to see his friends. It felt strange to have a celebration he would not be able to attend. Thanksgiving came around, and all I could think was, This is the last holiday I ever spent with my son.

I remember in detail that first Thanksgiving Day. I woke up convincing myself that I could handle a couple of hours with family. It was to be hosted at my grandparent's house just as it had been for many years before. I had agreed to make a contribution to dinner and felt obligated to make an appearance. Then a thought that broke my soul filled my mind.

Just a few yards away from the house where my family and I would gather to celebrate and fellowship would be my son. Unable to be seen, heard, or felt, in the little cemetery directly across the road. I felt intense physical pressure and sadness at that moment, so I made the decision to cancel my attendance.

And of course, when the winter season was upon us, I felt like the reincarnation of Ebenezer Scrooge. There was nothing for me to enjoy anymore, no reason for me to laugh. I had lost a life that was created within me, and I was never going to get it back.

As I grieved, I watched the outside world continue without me. Especially my daughter's life. Although she had experienced the same loss I had, and even some of the same emotional trauma, I watched her muster the strength to keep fighting to live. There were times she would plead with me to come to family events, stressing how much she and the rest of my family worried about and missed me. I wasn't ready. Her friendships blossomed; her interests deepened; and her drive to plan for a successful future brightened. She continued to excel in her academics and graduated high school with merit. Pride swelled within me seeing how she was able to grow in the face of such a great tragedy. With his passing not even two years behind her, she began her freshman year of college away from home. Even that seemed like a walk in the park from the outside looking in. So, as she thrived, I was holding on by a string to any semblance of life.

Meanwhile, depression had a firm grip on me. Therapy gave me some hope for recovery but eventually cost too much. Bills started to pile up to the point where I ended up living without electricity for two-and-a-half months. My job was flexible and considerate of my circumstances, but the pay wasn't keeping me afloat. While I could have found another job that would meet my needs, I was too afraid of having no control over my surroundings. I could become an emotional wreck at any given moment, and I didn't want to start a new job with a warning label attached to me. My new stressors mixed with the old wounds overwhelmed me to a point that I wanted to stop trying to bring my life back to normal. I no longer cared what anyone else thought about how much I was coming to terms or not. I no longer had my son and nothing else mattered.

I just about lost my fight when I was evicted just two years after burying my son. Unfortunately, it was no surprise; I had simply stopped trying to win a battle I felt I had already lost. I put on for others because I became tired of trying to get people to understand how difficult it felt to be happy when my son was not here to be happy too. I didn't want to explain anymore how guilty I felt about new experiences because my son would never have those experiences. It seemed like the hits kept coming, and I was the main character in the ultimate sob story.

WHEN I HIT THE RECORD BUTTON

I sat in my car that night, going through old pictures on my phone. Tears began to roll down my face as I took note of how my life changed over time. There was the youth league period. All three of us were involved, her a cheerleader, him a football player, and me a coach. Spring break vacations, first day of school pictures, birthday videos, and more pictures. I noticed that even back then there were pictures of me. Then came the series of photos after his death. There were fewer people and almost none of me. I only took pictures on a few special occasions, such as my daughter's graduation and her birthday, but there was one picture that stopped me in my tracks. It was the one that made me realize my son would be lost forever if I let myself go.

I stared at this picture of my baby girl on her graduation day, kneeling at her little brother's grave, with her cap turned towards the camera. She had decided to decorate the cap to her success and in the honor of his memory. It was also important to her to visit with him the day of her commencement ceremony because she wanted to share this experience with him. This was a milestone, and she made sure to make him as much a part of it as anyone else. That was when I knew I had to change my point of view. Even though I was experiencing tough times in the wake of a great loss, I needed to work on healing myself so I could get back on track to living.

I knew the healing process wouldn't be easy, and I knew every day would not feel terrible, but it was important to remember the days I felt good and be mindful of the days I didn't.

Looking through that digital photo album struck an idea within me. I was able to relive those experiences, through pictures and videos. I could see and hear what life was like in that moment. I've always considered myself a visual learner, and what better way could I learn about myself than by watching myself? At first, I thought it was a silly idea to create a video journal, but visualizing my emotions and the reasons why I was feeling that way would seem like it would be much more impactful. I figured most people never really see the changes within themselves because they see themselves every day. If I made it so that I was seeing myself as an outsider, maybe I could catch something that I would otherwise miss.

The first recording felt silly. I couldn't believe I was talking aloud to myself and recording it. I didn't think it would amount to much, but as soon as I opened my mouth, the words and thoughts came spewing out. It felt like a release of pent-up energy that I needed to purge. I can honestly say those feelings felt better out than they did when I held them in, especially for as long as I did. My expectation was not to go from zero to one hundred, and I knew that not every recording would be happy or positive. All I wanted was to be open and honest with myself.

While I still have no gauge on what emotions will arise, I can always look back and ask myself, What made me feel that way and why? Then the next time I face a similar situation, I can better navigate those emotions. Even if it is exploring them deeper in the same direction or finding an alternate solution to cope.

It is impressive to watch these videos sometimes because I can see my progress. I have watched life pouring back into me, and I am proud to hear the strength I have regained. While the sadness and anger are still there, I see it less and less. I am making the necessary changes to accept my new normal and reconnect with those who I care for and love. Working through my grief is something I may have to endure for the rest of my days, but with what I have learned, I will forever be indebted to my favorite daughter and my favorite son for helping me to live again.

Nine

Healing Through Paint

A Personal Journey About Grief

DANIELA DOHNERT

It was a usual August afternoon in 2010. After spending eight years studying and living in different parts of the world, I was back in my hometown of Caracas, Venezuela, and had been for the past ten years. Following my return from life in Hong Kong, Boston, and London, I decided to settle in the warm, colorful country I remembered from my childhood. A couple of years after returning to Venezuela, I met my husband, and by 2010, we had been married for five years.

That afternoon, I was walking through the familiar streets of my neighborhood, heading to the hospital to visit my gynecologist. I remember running into Matias, the man who sweeps the roads, and asked him how his family was. I was looking forward to the mangoes he dropped off at our house every week. Matias reminded me to look out for the holes on the sidewalk so I wouldn't trip.

At that time, I was six months pregnant with my third child and sensed that something was not quite right with the pregnancy. I hadn't felt my baby kick for a while and was concerned that I might be losing sensation in my body. The medication I was taking wasn't keeping my blood pressure under control; it never went below 140. The fear that something might change the future of my family overwhelmed me.

I had spent weeks preparing the house and family for baby Elena's arrival. A crib room was organized, and the two older children slept in the same room in preparation. This whole pregnancy had been different from the previous ones. I felt heavier, perhaps because of the high blood pressure or because I was unsure if I could be a good mother to three children instead of two. All the pregnancies had happened quickly after marriage, despite my efforts at birth control. I had become pregnant using an intrauterine device (IUD), and during lactation—Venezuelan lore says women don't ovulate during lactation. These were the only methods available to me as I have an allergy to latex and a history of blood clots, which took birth control pills out of the equation. I love children and caring for them but was scared of the energy necessary to have one more since I was already giving so much of myself to the first two.

I had decided, with my husband, to put aside my work as a teacher and artist to focus on raising our children. I was placing immense pressure on myself to be an outstanding mother. I felt I was letting my parents down by not pursuing my art career at all costs and not using any of the knowledge I gained from living abroad for close to a decade. At the same time, I wanted to ensure I gave my children all the physical affection and loving attention I felt my own childhood lacked.

My husband and I were renting the bottom floor of a house owned by my mother. I wanted to differentiate the way I raised my family from the way I was brought up; yet I was repeating the same patterns I had seen as a child. I, too, had grown up in my maternal grandmother's house, and my grandmother was the ultimate household authority. Don't get me wrong, having my parent's support was a lifesaver after my first daughter because I suffered from postpartum depression. However, it also placed some unspoken expectations in the environment as to how I should bring up my children.

When I think about that first postpartum depression, I think it originated from the self-imposed pressure for perfection and to make others proud. I told myself that since I was not working so I could care for my baby, I had to be outstanding at it. I worried about everything that related to my first daughter, from the color and consistency of her feces to how often she asked or did not ask for food.

Back then, I was on a vegetarian diet, which I had adopted years earlier as a consequence of watching Apocalypse Now while drunk in my high school sweetheart's dorm room. The image of the cow being decapitated was too much for me, and I became a radical vegetarian. That was a diet decision I made based on morality and not on health. I was oblivious to the protein requirements of the human body and didn't realize that although finding vegetarian options to eat was easy in the U.S. and England, those options were harder to find in Venezuela. My malnutrition was also impacting my health. I was a vegetarian eating mostly salads and unaware of the nutrients my body needed or received. I believe that also contributed to my postpartum depression. I was fortunate to realize I was depressed, and that is why my husband and I moved closer to my family, so I could be surrounded by people I knew.

Returning to that day in August 2010, I remember entering the doctor's office. He looked at me and asked, "What's wrong?"

"I haven't felt the baby move in a while," I explained.

He proceeded to run a check-up. I still recall the mixture of fear and sorrow I felt when the doctor informed me that he couldn't hear a heartbeat, and the ultrasound revealed that my baby had strangled herself with the umbilical cord. I had suspected something was happening but never imagined it was this. My blood pressure was also very high, so the doctor arranged for me to undergo induced labor as soon as possible in order to avoid further consequences on my health.

This physical anomaly was heartbreaking enough, but a particular male nurse's harsh words made it even more unbearable. As I underwent induced labor and asked if there was any way I could have prevented this, he callously remarked, "What did you expect? Of course, your baby died. You killed your baby by allowing your blood pressure to remain so high."

Those words pierced my soul, and the grief and guilt of having killed my daughter took hold of me. I was sure it was my fault she died. I could feel myself falling into a spiral of shame, sadness, and anger that was likely to throw me into depression once again. It became difficult to speak without crying uncontrollably. I felt guilty and alone.

HEALING INSPIRATION

One morning, after one of the many daily calls from concerned friends and family, I found myself once again answering questions that made my heart ache.

"I'm sorry, are you OK?" they would ask. "Can you take care of your kids? They need you."

Each call, each question, felt like a dagger twisting in a wound that refused to heal. Though I always responded politely, inside, I was filled with anger. How could they expect me to sweep the experience under the rug and move on as if nothing had happened?

Yes, I had two other healthy children, and yes, I loved them dearly, but the sadness was all-consuming. The guilt of feeling like a bad person, a bad mother, overwhelmed me. Amid this turmoil, an unexpected urge to paint took hold of me. I hadn't painted anything other than nursery walls since art school in 1994. But now, I felt an undeniable need to express myself through paint.

With what materials I had at home, I began my journey. I had buckets of colorful house paints. I went to the local hardware store, purchased some wooden panels, and locked myself in the guest room.

For a little over a week, I painted and cried, pouring my soul onto the panels.

I applied the paint by letting it pour in thin lines through makeshift paper funnels. It felt as if the paint poured directly from my body, each color a release of the pent-up emotions within me. I chose colors that spoke to my anguish: blood red, which symbolized the shame and pain I felt, and strong orange and ochre, reflecting the intensity of my grief. Those early days, the panels were dominated by these dark, hot colors.

As the week progressed, something within me began to shift. The colors on the panels started to change. Blues, greens, and purples began to dominate, indicating a move toward hope and acceptance. Though I had no formal knowledge of the psychological relationship between color and emotions, my instincts guided me. Looking back at those paintings, it's clear they reflected my journey from fear and depression to a place of healing. White spaces started to appear, symbolizing new possibilities and a fresh start.

In total, I painted ten large panels. The process was cathartic. The act of pouring paint became a medium through which I could channel my grief and begin to heal. Those intense days of painting allowed me to confront and accept my emotions. By the end of that week, I felt a newfound strength. I could be present for my children and once again find joy in their lives.

I also learned that paint, especially water-based paints like acrylics and watercolors, has the capacity to absorb our emotions, allowing us to transfer them out of our bodies. Today, I use this medium to help my clients access and express their feelings, just as it helped me navigate one of the darkest periods of my life.

LOOKING BACK

Fourteen years have passed since that fateful afternoon in August. My family has since immigrated to the United States, bringing along all those paintings that were born from my grief. They serve as poignant reminders of those intense feelings and the power of transformation. In recent years, I have modified some of the paintings, cutting them into smaller pieces, layering them with different colors, and adding fused glass elements. This ongoing transformation allows the paintings to evolve alongside me, mirroring the current emotions I experience every day.

When I remember the experience I had in that delivery room, it is still not a happy memory. Yet, thanks to that time I spent painting, I can speak about it now and recognize the profound connection I developed with my art as a result of the experience. Art has been a healing force in my life since childhood, helping me to overcome wounds, improve my self-esteem, and adapt to different environments. Drawing, welding, and performance art have all played a role in this journey, allowing me to overcome feelings of loneliness and the sense of not belonging.

If you are wondering how you can get started with painting, here is a quick guide on how to start. First, remember that painting only involves the act of putting paint on a surface; the subject of the painting and quality of it is relative to the viewer. We have all painted at some point during our early school years. When you are getting started with painting as an adult, put yourself in the shoes of a child. This is a way to make it fun and take the weight off of it.

Next go to a shop and purchase some water based tempera or finger-paint, craft paper or watercolor paper, and paintbrushes. At first, don't aim for anything expensive or fancy. This will allow you to experiment more readily.

Start by choosing three different colors of paint (A, B, and C), and paint a circle in the center of the paper with color A. Then make a ring outside the circle with color B, trying to blend the transition between the colors. Repeat the same with color C. This simple exercise can help you give into the colors.

For the blending process, try to mix the colors outside of the paper or painting watered down layers of color on top of each other. If you wish to take this a step further, after the paint is dry take a thin brush, choose a color that contrasts with A, B, and C. This color could be white or black if you haven't used them. With a thin brush, paint several curved lines that cut across the colored rings. You can repeat this same exercise with as many colors and shapes as you want.

Once you are comfortable with the use of color, take your painting to an outdoor space and paint a sort of landscape. Use only straight lines across the horizon to show the colors of the ground, sky, and anything else that is in front of you—whether it's the road, buildings, sea, fields or mountains. Make the thickness of the different colored lines relate to the approximate space those elements occupy in the landscape you are observing.

You do not need to add many details in the first layer, the details will come after this first layer of paint is dry. Once dry, take some more paint of the same colors or darker and lighter versions of them, and add any lines or blocks of color that will make your painting resemble more what you see. The purpose of this practice is not trying to make a photograph of the landscape but rather to bring forth the colors in this landscape that appeal to you.

These exercises will help you become comfortable with paint and when repeated often enough will open the doors to your creative expression.

Of all the mediums I have practiced, painting and writing offer the most immediate healing. They are accessible and require little preparation. Connecting with the colors that call out to us and allowing them to flow onto the canvas, or letting words pour out onto paper without censorship, is a wonderful way to express and release our troubled feelings.

As I reflect on these years, I realize how much art has been a lifeline. Those initial paintings, born from pain, have been transformed just as I have been. They stand as a testament to the resilience of the human spirit and the healing power of creative expression.

Ten

Heal Generations of Trauma

Moving Forward by Understanding Our Past

PALOMA GONZALEZ

Growing up, my mom was always working, which made me feel like I didn't matter. Even though she tried to be around when she could, her job and her troubled relationship with my father made things difficult. I often had to look after my younger brothers and try to fill in for her absence. The lies she told only made it harder to trust anyone in the family. Every day felt like walking on eggshells, never knowing when things would go wrong. These experiences were tough, and I often felt lost, just wanting to find a place where I belonged and had a purpose.

One vivid example of this chaos was how she manipulated the truth about her relationship with my dad. She would tell everyone that their marriage was falling apart because of his constant absence and lack of commitment. According to her, he was the root of all their problems, and she would paint herself as the victim who was left to pick up the pieces.

But behind closed doors, the reality was different. I would hear her and my dad arguing, with her making false accusations and blaming him for things that weren't his fault. It became clear that she was twisting the truth to create chaos and control the narrative. She would tell me stories about how my dad never cared about us, but then I'd see him making genuine efforts to be involved and supportive, only to be met with hostility and more lies from her.

The confusion and tension were overwhelming. I felt trapped in the middle, not knowing whom to believe or how to navigate the conflict. Her lies not only strained her relationship with my dad but also shattered the sense of security we all craved. Every argument, every half-truth, and every false accusation created a turbulent environment where trust and peace were nowhere to be found.

At sixteen years old, I found myself searching for my purpose in a world full of challenges that shaped my path. Every day felt like pieces of a puzzle that made me wonder where I fit in this world. I faced obstacles that felt overwhelming, trying to understand my purpose and find my way through life's difficulties.

THE SILENT LEGACY

I discovered the transformative power of neuro-linguistic programming (NLP) and trauma coaching. These tools helped me unravel my past, heal from my wounds, and see a clearer vision of my future. This journey not only helped me overcome my personal battles but also ignited a passion within me to help others do the same. It helped me realize that my purpose stems from empowering others to find their strength and resilience. Today, I use my experiences and expertise to guide individuals through their own journeys of self-discovery and healing, helping them unlock their full potential and thrive in life.

My journey of healing began with a profound understanding that the struggles I faced were not just mine alone but echoes of a history buried deep within my family. It was a revelation that unfolded over time, through stories passed down at family gatherings, whispered conversations, and moments of shared sorrow. Generational trauma is a silent legacy that shapes our lives in profound ways. It shapes our beliefs, influences our choices, and often manifests in ways we may not fully comprehend until we confront it head-on.

Growing up, I could feel the weight of my mother's silent struggles. In the quiet corners of our home, during moments of introspection, I often caught glimpses of her grappling with memories that seemed to weigh on her soul. Sometimes, her gaze would linger on old photographs adorning the walls, a testament to a past she rarely spoke about but carried with her every day.

There were also times when she found comfort in being alone, withdrawing to protect me from the deep struggles she faced. It was during these moments of quiet reflection that I began to piece together fragments of her narrative woven with threads of hardship, resilience, and unwavering determination. I came to realize her life was like a tapestry woven with challenges that I could only begin to understand. She had faced storms that rocked our family, unexpected situations, financial hardships that stretched our resources thin, and personal sacrifices made of love and necessity.

Each trial left its mark on her, shaping lines of strength and resilience in her face, a testament to her unwavering determination in the face of difficulties. Through it all, she bore the weight of her responsibilities with grace, navigating turbulent waters with a quiet determination that left an indelible mark on my own understanding of resilience. She had the ability to rise above challenges, to find light in moments of darkness.

As I grew older, I began to grasp the depth of her sacrifices. I saw the countless late nights she spent working to provide for our family, ensuring we had what we needed. I understood the compromises she made, sometimes setting aside her own desires to prioritize our well-being. I also saw the silent battles she fought, shielding us from the harsh realities of life with a quiet strength that spoke volumes. Her love served as a constant anchor in our lives, steadying us through turbulent times and reminding us of the enduring power of family bonds. In witnessing her perseverance, I learned not only the importance of resilience but also the profound impact of generational trauma.

I began to notice that certain behaviors were deeply tied to the trauma inherited from previous generations. Simple triggers, like a particular tone of voice or a lingering silence, created reactions that felt almost automatic, as if they were ingrained in me long before I fully understood their origins.

It was as though I was reliving experiences that weren't entirely my own but were instead echoes of my ancestors' pain. I would find myself responding to situations with fear, anger, or a need for control, even when the present circumstances didn't require such intensity. These patterns of behavior became a clear signal that the trauma had been passed down, manifesting in ways that shaped my relationships, decisions, and overall sense of self. Recognizing these triggers was the first step in understanding the depth of the generational trauma I carried. It allowed me to see how deeply rooted these patterns were and how they influenced my life in ways I hadn't previously realized. This awareness became the foundation for my healing journey, as I learned to uncover these reactions, understand their origins, and work towards breaking the cycle.

My journey of healing began with recognizing and understanding generational trauma, leading me to seek methods and practices that could break the cycle and foster true emotional freedom. My mother and I embraced the opportunity to rewrite our narrative and break free from the shadows of generational trauma. Each challenge brought new insights and revelations, allowing us to release the negative emotions that tethered us to the past and embrace a future rooted in resilience and understanding. As we navigate our shared history, I witnessed the transformative power of empathy and compassion.

Every reaction, every response, was like a thread leading back to a time when survival depended on being hyper-vigilant or withdrawing from self-protection. Acknowledging this was both humbling and empowering—it meant that we were not just passive recipients of our ancestors' struggles but active participants in rewriting our story. This awareness allowed us to approach our healing with greater intention, knowing that each step forward was not just for ourselves but for breaking the cycle for future generations. It was in these moments of clarity that we found the courage to challenge old beliefs, question automatic reactions, and replace them with healthier, more conscious choices.

Our conversations became a safe space where we could explore painful memories, unpack long held beliefs, and reshape our perspectives. It was a process of mutual healing, where each revelation deepened our bond and reinforced our commitment to supporting one another. There were moments of doubt and uncertainty, where old wounds threatened to resurface. Yet, with each setback, we leaned on the lessons of compassion, forging ahead with courage and determination. It was through this persistent effort we began to dismantle the patterns of the past, creating space for new, healthier ways of living and being. By embracing vulnerability and seeking support, we cultivated resilience, allowing us to transform pain into strength and create a legacy of healing and hope for future generations. Through it all, we found strength in our shared experiences and the knowledge we were not alone in our struggles.

My mother began to share her own journey of healing moments of self-discovery and personal growth. She shared stories of resilience and triumph, revealing the strength that carried her through life's darkest moments. Her courage inspired me to confront my own vulnerabilities and embrace the transformative potential within myself. Together, we confronted the ghosts of our past with courage and determination. We acknowledged how the wounds shaped our lives and committed ourselves to breaking the cycles of pain and suffering.

As we continued our path of healing, my mother's evolution, a woman who had once been defined by her struggles, now radiated with newfound confidence and inner peace.

BLAZING A NEW PATH

In embracing our truth and confronting our past, we have unlocked a reservoir of inner strength and resilience that continues to guide us forward. As we navigate life, we do so with a renewed sense of purpose and a commitment to fostering healing in ourselves and others. Our journey has taught me that healing is not a destination but a continuous process of growth and compassion. It has shown me the profound impact of acknowledging our vulnerabilities and embracing. Through it all, I have come to understand that our scars are not marks of weakness, but they serve as symbols of our courage to confront and transcend adversity. I am inspired by the possibilities that lie before us.

As we look towards the future, I feel gratitude for the journey that brought us to this moment of healing and transformation. Our story is a testament to the resilience of the human spirit, our capacity to overcome adversity, heal wounds, and forge a path toward a future guided by love, compassion, and hope. Reflecting on our shared journey, I see how each step we took towards healing has not only strengthened our bond, but it also illuminated the power of empathy and understanding. Our story is not just about personal healing but about breaking cycles of pain that persisted through generations. It is about reclaiming our voices, rewriting our narratives, and paving the way for a future where healing is accessible and transformative.

I carry with me the lessons of the importance of compassion, the strength found in vulnerability, and the power of forgiveness to heal even the deepest wounds. Together, my mother and I have reshaped our story from one of pain and struggle to one of resilience, growth, and boundless possibility. With this newfound understanding and healing, I am committed to leading others on their own journeys of transformation. I plan to use my experiences to guide those who are still navigating the shadows of their past, offering support and tools to help them break free from generational cycles.

This new perspective has become the foundation of how I live my life each day. It shapes how I interact with others, approach challenges, and make decisions, always with an awareness of the impact my actions can have on both me and those around me.

For instance, when faced with a difficult decision, I now take a moment to reflect on how it aligns with my values and goals. I consider not only how it will affect me but also how it will influence the people I care about. Recently, when a close friend was going through a tough time, I approached the situation with empathy and patience, remembering how important it is to offer support and understanding. Instead of reacting impulsively, I chose to listen deeply and provide thoughtful guidance, ensuring that my actions contributed positively to our relationship.

BREAKING THE CYCLE

Healing from generational trauma begins with acknowledging its presence in your life. Take time to reflect on the stories, patterns, and silent struggles that have shaped your beliefs and behaviors. As you do, allow yourself to feel the emotions that arise sadness, anger, or confusion. These feelings are valid and part of the process. Vulnerability is strength, and by embracing these emotions, you begin to release their hold on you.

Find a safe space to share your reflections, whether with a trusted friend, family member, or support group. Speaking your truth can provide relief and foster deeper connections. In sharing, you realize you are not alone, and through empathy, you gain strength.

With this awareness, you can rewrite your narrative. Envision a future shaped by resilience, love, and hope. Identify the strengths you've uncovered through challenges and use them to break free from the patterns of the past. Healing is not a destination but a continuous journey, one that requires patience and self-compassion.

By acknowledging your past, expressing your emotions, and crafting a new narrative, you can break the cycle of generational trauma. Remember, you are not walking this path alone, and the strength you find within will guide you toward a future of hope and healing.

This thoughtful approach has not only strengthened my connections with others but also enhanced my ability to navigate life's obstacles with grace and resilience. It's a daily practice of mindfulness and intentionality that helps me stay grounded and focused on my mission to uplift and inspire those around me.

I strive to create spaces of empathy and understanding, where people can feel safe to explore their own histories and find the courage to heal. By embodying the principles of resilience, compassion, and growth, I hope to inspire others to embrace their own power to change, contributing to shift towards a more compassionate and healed world.

Eleven

The Essential Unraveling

The Loss That Found Me

ELIZABETH SOTO-BAEZ

"**Y**ou're not listening!" I shouted.

Only weeks into being a wife and another argument. The rage within me was unfamiliar and before I could think, I had slammed our wedding champagne flutes on the counter breaking off the stems. My hands were bleeding and my crystal flutes were destroyed. Shame and disappointment enveloped me like a heavy cloak. The weight of it pulled me into an unrecognizable darkness.

What is happening? I know marriage is hard, but now? This soon? It's only been a few weeks, what am I doing wrong?

I looked at the engravings on the flutes, Mr. & Mrs, the memory of my wedding day flashing within me. Phoenix in October was still warm. A cloudless sky, red rock mountains in the background—I had always wanted an outside wedding. Pristine white chairs lined in rows in the beautiful garden waiting to greet friends and family who were over the moon for this union. As tears flowed down my cheeks, I smiled at the memory. It was the day I felt most beautiful.

I'm jerked back into reality; he's still shouting at me. A door slams.

What have I done? How do I escape this? Will it always be like this? Maybe it really is me? Maybe there's something I need to do to be better? What's wrong with me?

I stepped into my marriage with the full knowledge that it would require work. Coming from a family full of divorcees, I promised myself I'd **never** be a divorced person. I would do it "right." I would put in all the work, and I would win. How do you win at marriage? I didn't actually know, but that didn't matter; I was gonna make it happen somehow. I had a stellar track record for making things happen, and this would be no different.

I would make it happen.

I would show up.

I would do the work.

I would not let my marriage fail.

I would not be a divorced person. Divorce was never going to be an option.

I was twenty-three, and it was this promise that paved the road to losing myself.

Let's go back to May 2019. I woke up that day with my heart pounding, my breath shallow and labored. This was the day, the day that I told my husband I could no longer be married.

My heart ached. *How did it come to this?* Life was moving around me, and I was stuck in slow motion, thirteen years of marriage racing through my mind.

What happened to me? Where did I go? Who am I, really? Why have you never seen me? Known me? Questions I had been asking myself for weeks now echoing in my mind as I dragged myself through the morning willing myself to be as normal as I could.

How do you act "normal" when you realize you gave yourself up for a promise that was impossible to keep? How do you gather yourself up once more to act as other people want when you finally see that you've been nothing for yourself?

Feelings buried alive don't die. I read that on social media years before, and it was the first glimpse into the realization, "I'm lying to myself." And on this day, preparing to end my marriage, a volcano of emotions erupted within me. Years of work hiding them in the depths of my being, and today they came rushing through like river rapids. They could no longer be contained. As much as I made myself believe what I felt didn't matter—it wasn't true. All of me, feelings, thoughts, experiences, fears, joys, it all mattered. It was time to embrace myself.

I do matter.

That morning I called out of work. I told Matt, my husband at the time, that I had a migraine and was going to stay home. At this, he asked me to please help get our boys ready for school (they were seven and nine years old at the time) and then proceeded to blend his morning smoothie. The blender whirring just feet away from me and my migraine, it was another stark realization: I don't matter. What I feel doesn't matter. What I need doesn't matter. My migraine was an obvious inconvenience and of no consequence.

Matt left to take our sons to school, and I spent the day in waves of panic and fear. *How do I do this? What do I even say? What will he say?* I didn't know a single thing about how to calm my body or how to hold myself. I just needed to tell him and also, *Oh god, I have to tell him!*

We had plans to have dinner that night with some friends, and when he checked in midday, I suggested he cancel them.

"I still have a migraine." I texted.

He responded, "Well, why don't you just stay in the bedroom, and I'll just stay with Megan and Rob."

Another dagger to a heart already shredded by years of neglect and gaslighting.

You're not really important. We can't inconvenience our friends with your migraine, so you just stay away and I'll hang out with our friends. You'll be fine. No biggie. This is what I felt.

I was once again...invisible.

I sat with myself, counting down the hours in both dread and anticipated relief. In those hours of waiting, I took myself on a journey. What was this last thirteen and a half years, really?

I walked into this marriage with the naivete of any young twenty-something. Elated at the joy of finding "the one" to spend all my years with. We would build our lives—travel, cook, read, snuggle, laugh, dream, explore—we had so much in common. We wanted so many of the same things, and it would be a dream (cue heart bubbles, unicorns, and rainbows).

Then within just weeks of marriage, I stood in stark awareness that this indeed was not what I imagined. My immediate thought was, *I can make it better. I can only change myself and I will, I will do this.*

Except no amount of reading, therapy, prayer, venting, ignoring, reframing, or apologizing changed a single thing. Nothing. Scanning my life in those hours of waiting, I spent thirteen years swimming against the current, pushing myself, like a chameleon hoping that a change in me would spark a change in him, in us. It didn't. Becoming a seen, connected, loved, appreciated, respected, and accepted partner would never happen.

I was a shell of a human. I was empty, hollow. Whatever had once been beautiful and good could no longer be found. Unable to control the sobs and waves of grief and sadness that overtook, I could hear his voice reminding me.

Weeks before I had reconnected with a high school friend. It had been twenty years since we had last spoken and, as old friends do, we reminisced about the joys and challenges that came with high school life. We also shared what was new, what had transpired in the two decades since our last contact. Listening as he shared stories about me and his memories brought me to my knees in sadness. I was no longer that girl.

I could hear him saying, "Don't you remember? Everyone loved you; you volunteered and you sang. You were on student counsel and everyone wanted to be like you. You were the smartest girl in school. And look at you, doing everything you said you would do, that is so amazing!"

"What?! Who are you talking about?" I remember saying in response.

I don't know this girl. I didn't remember her, but as he shared, a flicker, the tiniest of sparks ignited again within me. *She's still in there.* That girl who loves on others, who sets goals and reaches them, who is ambitious and won't be held back, who makes people smile and conquers all. She's still in there.

The time to tell Matt was drawing closer, and I knew without a shadow of a doubt that this was it. He didn't know me and honestly, neither did I. It was my work now, to find me again. To fan the flame within that once again flickered.

It was time to find that girl who would change the world, starting with her own.

No more hollow living. No more survival. No more shame. No more sadness. It was time to launch into a new life.

Making the choice to step out of my marriage despite a promise I made to myself and my husband, and in opposition to what others thought (or might think!) was crazy hard. There is no way around it. It was awful. Here's the truth: No one lived my life but me. No one knew my story or carried my weight, so when it was time to choose what people expected or what I needed to breathe and be alive...I chose me.

If you find yourself living in a similar situation, I see you.

"How did you do it?" was a question I received and nearly blindsided me after ending my marriage. Women in my life who had heard about my separation called me.

"How did you do it? Were you scared? How are you doing, really? I think I need a divorce too, but how?"

My immediate reaction was, *What the...?! Who am I to answer these questions? What do I have to offer?* And then, I knew. *It's not just me. This isn't just me!*

One of the biggest lies we tell ourselves as humans is that we are the only ones, and the truth is we are never the only ones. Women hide behind the facade of marriage, pretending, smiling while dying inside. This can't happen anymore, not if I can do something to spark change. It was my launch into the life of healing, not just for myself but offering to be a companion on the healing journeys of other women. On this journey, I've discovered five integral components that have served as a compass for me and my clients.

Number one was to embrace self-care. Pouring from an empty cup was my default; no wonder I felt like I was constantly dragging myself through the mud. Understanding that taking care of my needs first was going to spill over into the lives of my children and other loved ones was a challenge, and also worth the effort. Starting small is perfect. At the beginning of my journey, one of my favorites was audio books and walks. So nourishing for my body, mind, and soul.

What is one self-care routine you can integrate into your life now?

Taking care of myself quickly became a non-negotiable, as was finding my people, my second lesson. Healing happens in relationships, and it's time to find those humans in your life who are safe, and who will love you on your great days and on your hard ones. I call my divorce the "Great Sifter" because those who were about me stayed, and those who weren't left. It was okay, and I'm grateful. I would not be where I am today without those humans who have loved me through.

Who is one person you can count on in this season?

Rediscovering fun was another component I came to welcome as a requirement for healing. We become adults and suddenly lose sight of fun for fun's sake. Engaging in fun releases all those yummy brain chemicals we need. You **get** to have fun, and the only person who can give you permission is you! If deciding what's fun feels hard, consider what was fun when you were a kid and remember: It doesn't have to be fun for anyone but you!

What is one activity that you find fun that you can schedule today?

Number four on my list of healing components is what I call a "life audit." It's time to review how you spend your time. What's taking up most of your "life"? The truth is your time **is** your life. Most of us complain that we don't have "time," but once you review how you spend your time, you realize maybe some things need to change. And a reminder for you: Be gracious. This part of healing will require you to take notice in a way you may not have done before and that's okay. You can do it.

What is something that you can remove from your calendar? How can you make time for what you want most?

My last must-have in this healing and rediscovery is finding the right professional. Sometimes all the books, podcasts, girls nights, and self-care can't spark the change and healing we need. Finding the right professional to join your tribe is often an integral part of healing and moving on. Breaking cycles, stopping painful patterns, and eliminating self-sabotage often takes the support of someone outside of yourself, someone who is both for you and will be objective in their perspective. I often joke that my therapist was the bestie I paid to listen to me. We laughed about it because well, it was kinda true!

What professional do you need to invite into your life to provide support on this healing journey? A coach? A therapist? Both?

My divorce was the loss that found me. The brokenness that built me.

You're not stuck, unless you decide it is so.

It's time to launch your life—whatever age or stage, you can launch.

How will you launch your life?

Twelve

From a Mistake to a Masterpiece

A Journey of Healing

RAE WOODWARD

I love coffee! I started drinking coffee when I was five years old, thanks to my grandma. People told her, "Don't give her coffee, it will stunt her growth!"

Well thank you, Grandma, because at the age of fourteen, I was five feet, eleven inches! If not for grandma's coffee, I'd probably be well over six feet tall!

However, my first memories aren't of coffee, but of my dad screaming, breaking things, pushing me away from him, and passing out. He was an alcoholic. My young mind believed it was my fault when he behaved this way.

Why did he push me away? Why is he yelling? Something must be wrong with me. I was terrified of my dad and learned at a very early age how to walk on eggshells.

When I was six years old, my dad accepted Christ as his Savior, and he never drank again. However, life and his moods weren't always great. Looking back, I realize he still had so much to work through, but back then, damage was already done and my trust in him was gone.

Despite some painful early moments, I also have many happy memories growing up. I am the oldest of four kids and grew up in Tampa, Florida. I was an excellent student in school, had lots of friends, took piano lessons, bossed my younger siblings around—all typical growing up stuff. But between my height, glasses, braces, and a first name none of the other girls had, I knew I was not cool. I always felt like an outsider and had to prove my worth. I felt like I never measured up no matter how hard I tried. I was a mistake and convinced God made a poor choice when He made me.

Those feelings intensified as I became a teenager. Insecure in every way a teenager can be, I knew I had to change something. Why not try smoking weed? Some cool kids in our neighborhood were smoking, and they had been asking me to try it, so I did.

My parents found out, and it did not go well. Dad wanted to kick me out of the house, but I think that's illegal when you're in the eighth grade, so instead I was grounded for a long time. Meh, whatever. I kept smoking and tried a few more things. However, I made sure I didn't get caught again. This apathy led to years of poor choices, and I have the scars to prove it. I was damaged goods, unworthy of grace—God's or anyone else's.

In the fall after high school, I moved to Bloomington, Indiana, to stay with my uncle so I could "find myself". Within two months of being there, I met Curt. He liked to party too, but he was different. He was kind and respected me. What was that about? After a month of dating, he asked me to marry him. I laughed and told him I would let him know. After three months of dating, we moved in together. Yes, I was "living in sin" as my parents put it, but they were the least of my concerns. Curt and I were growing closer. Curt brought his own baggage to our relationship but we let the pain of our childhoods bond us together more. We just got each other. We were really building a life together, and it felt great to be accepted for me—flaws and all.

Then I found out I was pregnant. Gulp. Immediately I went into panic mode. *What should I do? I'm still a kid so I can't possibly raise a kid!*

Curt had said from the beginning he wanted to marry me, but I didn't know if I even loved this guy, let alone marry him. On the flip side, if I move back home, my parents would kill me. I had been doing a lot of drugs too, so this pregnancy would be high risk. Yes, this was yet another mess up from God's mistake, but in the end, I couldn't bear the thought of facing my family, so I had an abortion. I knew Curt was disappointed and I felt bad about that, but once it was done, it was easy to shut off my brain and emotions, and I stopped thinking about it. Party on!

Curt and I continued to grow more in love, and three years later I finally said "yes" to his proposal. He provided me with the unconditional love and acceptance I had been yearning for, and I knew I wanted to spend the rest of my life with him. My relationship with my parents was starting to get better, but I was still insecure around them and wasn't sure if they ever approved of Curt, so we eloped.

In an effort to begin a life as a normal married couple, we relocated closer to my parents. As it turned out, Curt and my dad got along great. It had been years since I had any major conflicts with my parents, but I was cautious around them.

Around this time, I started thinking about God. I was married now, so my wild partying days needed to be behind me. I started going to church, but my spiritual growth was slow. So much of me felt like I didn't belong there. I was still riddled with resentment and guilt. Even though I had asked Jesus into my heart when I was a child, I was convinced I was a mistake. *How could God love me after all the wrong things I had done?*

However, true to God's nature, slowly and ever so gently He began talking.

One afternoon, I picked up a devotional, and it seemed as though God was speaking directly to me. I heard a whisper in my ear that said, "What are you doing?" I knew it was God talking and I instantly broke. It was a revelation and I surrendered. It was time for a change in how I moved forward in life.

We welcomed our first son about five years later. It was incredible, and we were overjoyed with being parents. Curt and I had never been closer; I was getting closer with my parents; we had steady jobs. Life was good!

A few months later I wanted to volunteer at our local crisis pregnancy center. I went through their training program, and on the second night, they described in detail what happens during an abortion. I had never wanted to hear this information. The remorse was overwhelming. Afterwards I broke down and wept. I asked God and Curt to forgive me, and for the first time in my life, I felt true grace. *Was this the start of some healing?*

Less than two years later, we had our second son, and life kept moving forward. We were in a good zone. Curt started going to church with me, and we were growing in our faith together. Things were cozy. All the pain of my past was behind me, or so I thought.

One day Curt did something that annoyed me. I can't remember what it was, but it triggered me, and I felt such intense rage that it scared me. *Where did that come from?*

I called my mom, and she told me to talk to a counselor as there could be trauma from my childhood I never dealt with. This suggestion kickstarted a three-year journey of facing my past, which included forgiving those who hurt me and accepting accountability and forgiving myself for those I hurt. It was hard, but it was necessary in order to be free. And it was time to confront my dad.

I didn't hold back. I had so much pent-up resentment towards him for thirty-some years that I couldn't hold my feelings in any longer. I told him about the fear of him when he was an alcoholic, and the judgment from him after he became a Christian. He failed me. I was terrified because I wasn't sure how he would react, and I was bracing for impact. However, he started crying and told me that I was right; he had failed me and wasn't the dad I needed. He asked me to forgive him and if we could start over and have a healthy relationship. I knew the grace God had given me, I needed to give my dad. That day everything changed for me. God began repairing our relationship and healing my soul. Three years later, we lost him to cancer.

Focusing on our own family, Curt and I developed a rhythm in life and it was going well. We still had our young eccentric spirits and loved to shower that part of us onto our kids. To us, our two sons and only daughter were going through the normal aches and pains every kid goes through growing up, and any trouble they got into was to be expected.

However, when our boys were nineteen and eighteen, we found out that they had been sexually abused when they were small children by a babysitter for months and had repressed the memories all those years. I cannot begin to describe the punch to the gut that was delivered. Not only was I devastated for my children, but the guilt I felt in not knowing and hiring that babysitter was crushing. I should have known, I should have seen signs. I had failed them completely. *How can any of us ever recover from this?*

We got them into counseling immediately, but remembering how I carried so much pain with me from my own childhood, I knew this was going to be a very long and difficult road to recovery for them. The impact it had on our entire family has been crippling. For me, I've had to navigate through this pain to find the balance of being their support and being their mom. This included an ocean of tears, panic attacks, and lots and lots of prayer.

About a year later, we discovered that our oldest child had been suffering from dissociative identity disorder and then came out to us as transgender. This was completely uncharted territory for me. I deeply struggled with that revelation and didn't know how to resolve the struggle. We raised him in a Christian home, and he had other Christian influences in his life. *Where did we go wrong? There is nothing that could ever make me stop loving him, but what do I do now?*

This was way too big for me to manage, so I took it to God. After talking about it and crying for what seemed like weeks, He told me something I remember so clearly, "I don't care about Graham's gender, I care about Graham's soul."

The peace I felt after hearing those words was supernatural, and that peace is what I focus on walking this path with my child. I never felt like I got grace from my parents growing up, and I was not going to do that to Graham. Curt and I had some serious talks, and we were on the same page. We would learn all of this together.

A few years later, Curt started having serious health issues. After some tests, we received the devastating diagnosis of terminal cancer. Although we fought as much as we could, it was too late for him to recover. In less than four months, he was gone. After thirty-five years together, I had lost my best friend, my partner, my person, my soul. He was my one constant through these never-ending hills and valleys. It is impossible to describe the depth of grief and sadness I felt. I never thought in a million years I'd have to do life without him. There was really no reason to go on, and I didn't want to. Life was simply just too hard.

Despite the overwhelming despair, with our daughter only being thirteen, I thrust myself back into mom mode right away. She needed me to be strong and responsible. In addition, our second child dove headfirst into alcoholism and got himself into trouble. I wanted to crawl under a rock for the next sixty years, but he was putting his life at risk. I couldn't abandon him, and I still felt like I was making up for his robbed childhood. I had to put grieving aside and stand as the pillar my family required.

How much, God? How much can I take?

As much as I wanted to fall back into that, "I don't deserve love" mindset, I chose to rely on God for my mere survival, even my next breath. I didn't have the strength to hold on to Him, but He held tightly on to me. God became more real to me than ever during this time and held me up when I couldn't go on. I cannot imagine what life would be like now if I had turned the other way.

Being on my own, what now? How do I support myself?

I partied my whole childhood away and spent my adulthood as a wife and mother. I'm almost sixty years old, and I'm starting over with almost no marketable skills. The Bible says that God promises to take care of widows and orphans, so I guess I qualify, but what can God do with someone like me?

I've read such fantastic stories in the Bible of God taking broken people and doing amazing things through them, but I never thought that would happen to me. However, he has guided me through a new chapter in life and made it abundantly clear that I have a story to tell, and I can help others with it. Through God's grace, wisdom, and provisions, I am proud to be a certified life and health coach, a mastery and transformational life coach, and a Clarity Catalyst Trainer. God is using me to help others transform their lives. What a fulfilling new purpose I've been given and what a privilege!

Each of us has our own journey, and God never promises us an easy life. Looking back, I'm amazed I'm still alive. But I am not a mistake, I am a masterpiece—fearfully and wonderfully made by a majestic and loving God. He has protected me, forgiven me, redeemed me, healed me, and strengthened me. He still has things for all of us to do; all we need to do is let go and let Him guide us.

Thirteen

Waiting for Perfect

Understanding My Authentic Self

MAEGEN MORRISON

I sat here for days trying to figure out how to start this chapter. Married to an alcoholic for seven years, then into another marriage with a narcissist for twenty years, and that's just to show you a little of where I came from and what I've overcome. I wondered if I should go back all the way and talk about my childhood and some of the generational issues in my life, which caused false perceptions in the way I looked at life, how I should live, who I should be.

As I wrote and deleted, wrote and deleted, I decided we all have been through life, and if you're reading this book, you're looking for inspiration and help. That's why you picked it up! In a bit, I'll highlight more about the healing journey and the mindset change that is needed in our lives to make the change, but let's go back to my story.

A WILD RIDE

Approximately four years ago, although my entire life has been a wild ride, I was married to a man in a motorcycle club, and I still ride a Harley myself. I've done and seen some stuff. I worked in the mining industry, which is definitely a man's world, for nineteen years running heavy equipment. I considered myself a strong female. However, I never realized the healing journey is the one I needed to strap in for!

After I finally left my second ex-husband and didn't go back, I stayed a little wild and did what I call "fake healing," which is just covering up all my emotions. I would go on trips and buy things. I started doing a lot of yard work and built a fence, put in a patio, built benches, and hung out with my friends. Staying as busy as I could, I put on this fake smile of being a happy, independent, single woman, but at the end of the day when things went silent, my thoughts were still there. My depression and anxiety reared their ugly heads. No matter where I went or what I did, I was still there with all my insecurities and fears. I could not run away from them no matter how far I went, no matter how far I buried them within me.

Fun note: During this time, I started a program to become a certified life coach. I've always been the person others came to for help or advice no matter how messy my life was. I decided I might as well get paid for it.

Plus, I really enjoyed helping others. It was a passion of mine. *If I couldn't help myself, I could at least help others*, I thought.

This course was amazing, and I would soon see I needed it for me more than I needed it to help others. Lesson by lesson it triggered all these unhealed traumas. The good part is I was given tools to overcome them and a wonderful partner in the course where our practice life coach training was not role-playing. These scenarios were very real.

I graduated from the Health Coach Institute, and I am now a certified health and life coach. I was very proud of this achievement and ready to conquer the world. Well, not quite yet.

GETTING TO KNOW THE NEW ME

Life started to hit pretty hard. My savings started to dwindle down, and there was no way I could get enough clients to pay my bills in time before it ran out, so I started a job search back to mining—the only thing I really knew. Let me set the scene.

Between getting certified and going back to work, I had isolated myself. I stopped going out; I was just focused on my training and my own healing. Soon after I got certified, I had a supernatural spiritual awakening. Proceed with caution, I'm going to be honest and vulnerable with you.

Things got messy and just plain crazy. My search for God began as well. I read the Bible from front to back four times and had multiple studies filling up notebook after notebook, studying multiple religions and beliefs. I always believed there was a God, but I was raised in a strict religion and left when I was eighteen years old. I got deep, and so you understand how deep, my son later told me he was scared that I may join a cult. I laugh about this now.

I had spent three out of four years searching for the truth. At one point I said, "What am I going to do with my life coach certification?"

I can't take the work of God away and felt that everything was just scripture re-worded. I believe it's important to believe in a higher power working on your behalf. I mean Jesus never healed anyone; their belief and faith did. I cannot emphasize enough how powerful your thoughts are!

Your inner beliefs will show up in your outside world. You will attract what you think about.

This leads me into "waiting for perfect". Here I am starting a new mining job that happens to be three hours away from home, so I pack up and leave my dogs and home for four to five days at a time, then return home for four to five days. That's the way the mining schedule works.

I was staying at a very low-end motel, and it was so bad I would cry myself to sleep most nights. I was an emotional wreck; it had been just me and my dogs and my twenty-something-year-old son at home for a year.

After the divorce, I had isolated myself from the world, aside from a wild four months or so. I rarely dated. I stopped hanging out with people, and I even stopped talking to my family for the most part. I needed time to find myself. It wasn't personal, but I married at eighteen and divorced after seven years, then jumped into another marriage for twenty years—the whole time hanging onto the beliefs of my family. Although I have always been a black sheep, I can honestly say I had no clue who I was or what I wanted from this life. I had always lived my life the way people needed me to.

Going back to work was very hard on me. Isolation is good for some things, but it can also give you a false sense of healed. It's easy to feel healed when you don't have any outside sources triggering your traumas. I gave myself a false sense of peace, but it wasn't a healthy way. Eventually, you have to step out and face the world and everything it throws at you. So I went out into the world again armed with a life coach certification and the word of God. What could go wrong, right?

Here I was working and saving, so I could live the dream and do my dream job when those words, *What could go wrong?* shouted as if to say, *Well, let me show you!*

Going back to the mining industry triggered me due to how I was treated and fired from the last one. My youngest son was sent to prison, serving nine to twenty years (still fighting this in 2024), and I started dating a guy. Since I had not been in a relationship for three years, this also hit some sensitive areas and triggered many past relationship traumas. This is when I got into my head and told myself, *How in the hell could I ever be a life coach when my life is such a mess? I need to do more work on myself, heal more, and get my life together before I can help others. I need to be perfect and then I can follow my dream.*

At one point, I gave up on it all together. Throughout the process, I noticed when I would get upset at something someone would do or say at work. I did react instead of respond, but less than an hour later, I asked myself, *Why did that upset me? Why am I so angry? Where the hell did that come from?*

I would ponder for a short while and understand where the trigger derived from, and I would talk to the individual, apologize, have a good conversation with them, and we worked through it. Right there is major growth. In the past, I would stay angry for days or months and let these things ruin my entire day. I was literally letting people control my mood. Now I know how to work through the process and even if something upsets me, I move past it quickly. My life coaching taught me it's about progression not perfection.

I started thinking about every situation that triggered me and instead of reacting right away, I would ask myself, *Why am I upset?* and *Was it worth my energy to even respond?*

Ninety-nine percent of the time it's not worth my energy, so I might shake my head, turn up my music, smile, and continue my job. Now that's some progress, and I'm pretty proud of myself.

The mining industry is like being back in high school. It's full of cliques and gossip, and a lot of ego-driven individuals. I do my best to stay out of it because it is very low energy and drains my energy. We all joke with each other and tease from time to time, but I like to leave the rest. It's not for me anymore, and I can say I'm doing well at rising above that low-vibe mentality. We all have to remember there is no such thing as perfect, and each and every situation teaches us something, or it can tear you down. Choose to learn and grow. I promise you it's a better way.

DECONSTRUCTING OLD BELIEFS

Now let's dive into my first relationship after not dating anyone for three years. I knew this guy for two years and worked with him, and I always thought he was a great guy—very kind and sweet, but he was married. I was not looking for a relationship at this time, so I never had those kinds of feelings for him. A while later, I found out he was having issues in his marriage, and I explained to him how important communication was, and he needed to talk to her about his feelings so they could both work on it together.

The next time I saw him I found out she packed up and moved out. I felt bad, but at the same time, I believe if love was strong enough, anything can be worked through, and I believed she had checked out long ago mentally and was waiting to physically leave.

Our friendship continued. Then one day there was a sudden shift in energy–a spark between us–this crazy connection I couldn't deny. In my head I was like, *This is crazy.*

I never knew how old he was, but he seemed older, like he had an older soul. When I realized he was way younger than me, I practically spit my drink out and thought, *Yeah, this will never work.* I was keeping my heart at bay, but this energy was so powerful and magnetic that no matter what I told myself, I couldn't deny it.

I let go of all fears and jumped in head first. We had the most beautiful time together. It was like we had known each other for a lifetime. Everything was amazing until the fears I held onto ruined a beautiful opportunity. This is why it's so important to heal, learn from your traumas, and be aware of them. I became aware of triggers, and I communicated everything to him.

The more communication and understanding, the more uncomfortable he was because the relationship became more real and not just a fantasy.

However, this man was not used to communicating or sharing emotions, but he would open up and share things he had never talked about before—from his childhood to the present day. He used to say, "This is like a romance movie, it's not real."

We mirrored each other's traumas and started triggering each other, which showed me the areas I needed to work on, and because of my training and spirituality, I was grateful for him. On the other hand, he saw these things as toxic and didn't understand them. All he knew is that he needed to suppress his feelings and emotions that bubbled up and made him feel too vulnerable. This is where he started to sabotage the entire relationship, which broke my heart for him.

He would say he wasn't worthy enough to be with me; he thought he could never be on "my level". He had basically come to the conclusion that he wasn't good enough for me, and I was way out of his league, and I would eventually leave him once I realized it. To spare himself humiliation in the future, he would end it—that way he had the illusion of controlling his pain before someone else caused it.

As humans, we look through different lenses. Some grotesque because we view things from our past experiences, our fears. His lenses were clouded, so any advice was taken as criticism or "I'm not good enough."

I removed all my boundaries for him and allowed myself to go back to old patterns by walking on eggshells so he wouldn't get upset or triggered. I put my life aside again to try to prove my love and completely forgot my own worth trying to save him. Even though I went into the relationship with a secure attachment style, his avoidant attachment style triggered me into my anxious attachment style. I was getting blamed for my reactions to his toxic behavior but could never talk about the disrespect that triggered it.

There's nothing wrong with giving people chances and understanding them with unconditional love, as long as we don't remove healthy boundaries we've set for ourselves. We can't control others' actions; we can only control the way we respond/react to them. Although this hurt my heart, it was a huge learning experience, and I understood what I was doing and recognized it in order to grow.

What we have to realize is unless someone is willing to face their traumas and take accountability for their actions to heal, they can't be forced. You can give them the tools and support, but you can't make them use them. I will always cherish this man and the things I learned in this relationship, and I have faith he will know his worth someday so he doesn't continue hurting others or himself.

To grow, we must change our lenses, our perception, deconstruct old belief systems, and remember nothing in this world has meaning unless you put meaning to it. Thoughts create beliefs, which create your reality. You don't have to be perfect; you just need to have the tools and faith to overcome any situations life brings.

Fourteen

The Unexpected Journey

Navigating Conflict, Healing, and Personal Growth

NEYSA LEWIS

Most people are excited about their birthday. For the most part, I am too. I am always happy to celebrate another year. The gift of life is not one I take lightly. The organization that I'm a part of loves to show their appreciation for me. In fact, they celebrate my birthday all month. It's an honor that they care and want to show it.

One would think I'd look forward to the attention during this special time of year. However, that's not really the case. As my birthday approaches, I always feel a bit of anxiety. There is usually arguing over whose idea is the best or who is responsible for certain tasks. Each year the disagreements get more intense. The division continues to grow. Instead of experiencing celebration and love, I often feel like I cause contention.

To my surprise, this particular year was not like that. I had a lot going on in my personal life. I was dealing with some health issues and had been out of work due to surgery. So, if there was bickering, I was not aware of it. I knew they were planning something; I just didn't know what. One day I received a call and was informed that nothing had been mentioned, and the caller was not sure if everyone was coming together like they usually do. She asked what she could do for me. I told her she could do whatever she wanted, and gift cards or cash would be just fine.

Everyone who knows me knows I plan things. At this time, it's March. My birthday is in April. Sometimes the organization gives specific amounts of money they would like each person to give. I didn't think there was enough time to place that kind of demand on them. Instead, I wanted my colleagues to do what they could and not feel pressured or embarrassed. It's the thought that counts, and I would show gratitude for anything they could do.

When I was released from bed rest, I returned to service. That day they announced they were in fact doing something for me. Others were informed of the plan, and they only had a week or two to send their contribution. I was then asked if I wanted to make any additional announcements.

They were glad to have me back and wanted to hear from me. Before I returned, I had received several phone calls from others who wanted to do something for me. Of course I told them the same thing—I would be grateful for whatever they could give or decide to do. Well, when I was given the microphone during service, I reiterated those things. That's when things took a turn. My announcement caused a huge explosion.

I'm exaggerating, but it did feel like an explosion. I found out that the leaders had been planning something all along. They were not happy with me giving the people an option that contradicted what they had already decided.

I didn't think it was a big deal. I was so wrong! It was a huge deal. The leaders were upset and felt I undermined them. I explained it was not my intention to undermine. I didn't tell the others not to participate. I had simply just given the members who were concerned with the short time frame another option. This caused the biggest divide in the organization that we have ever experienced. I couldn't figure out or understand why.

To me, I should be able to celebrate my birthday how I wanted. I don't take it lightly and know they go out of their way to make me feel special. If others show their love, then they should be able to do it the way they want. I expressed all of that. I even shared my gratitude for the thought and all the hard work they did. I thought that was the end of it. I was wrong again!

One day I received an email from one of the leaders who was also an assistant of mine. The email caught me completely off guard. She let me know that she had taken the things I said about the organization and planning personally. I apologized and explained again that my intent was not to offend her. I just knew that time and space would ease the tension surrounding my birthday.

A few weeks later, the leaders were in a class online. They were discussing things that make an effective ministry. I'm not sure how, but the incident was brought up and used as an example. This caused everyone to share their thoughts and feelings about my announcement and remarks. One thing led to another, and this class turned into a debate.

There was so much yelling. Some of the leaders stepped down. A lot of comments about me and my birthday were made. They were not good comments. I learned that day who all I upset when I gave my alternate suggestion. Some said I couldn't think for myself, and I was "being a puppet."

To top it off, I wasn't even on the call. The call was happening in my house, so I heard everything. All the explaining and apologizing I had done made no difference. Things had only gotten worse. I also learned that my husband agreed with my assistant and was upset as well.

It brought me back to my initial anxiety surrounding my birthday. I always hated feeling like such a special occasion could bring on so much strife. I never wanted to cause negativity. This time, though, they blamed me for the rift that had been caused. I attempted to communicate how I felt and how all the chaos made me feel. I understood the offenses for which I had repeatedly apologized to no avail. However, no one was trying to understand or listen to how I had been affected. It made me feel like I'm just expected to smile and be okay with however I am treated. Year after year, I stated how I did not like the behavior around my birthday. None of that was taken into consideration. I felt discarded and overlooked.

This story isn't to point a finger at anyone. I don't believe there was really a right or wrong. Each person had their reasons and felt justified in their actions and thoughts. I believe their motives and intentions were good. When feelings are involved, things get heated and cause others to act in ways they would not normally act. This incident made me second guess everything about myself, what I was doing, and how I was doing it. This situation revealed to me an area that still needed healing. I had some things within me that I needed to work through even though I thought I had. This crisis showed there were layers to my healing.

RECEIVING MY BLESSING

As a life coach, grief recovery specialist, and a leader, I realized that I didn't do what I told my clients to do. I needed to take an emotional evaluation. *What was I feeling at that moment?*

While emotions start as sensations in the body, feelings are generated from our thoughts about those emotions. In other words, feelings are how we interpret emotions. We use the word "feel" for both physical and emotional states. I didn't acknowledge what I was feeling.

I didn't allow myself to sit with my emotions and identify what was taking place within me during those difficult moments. I had to remind myself that it was okay to feel. It was time for me to take my own advice and evaluate my state of mind and my feelings.

What was I feeling? Why did I feel the way I did? What about the situation caused the negative feelings?

The more I thought about it, the more I began to think that there was no way God could use me broken. Not only was I broken, but as I began to navigate this journey, I realized I was also blind. I had no idea how I had gotten here or what was next. As I began to evaluate my emotions and thoughts, my feelings became more vivid. Anxiety set in. Frustration ran rampant. Disappointment was at an all-time high.

Was I disappointed in myself or God? Why did God allow me to feel the way I was feeling?

I replayed the scenario in my head attempting to figure out what could be done or said differently. I couldn't figure it out. The more thought I gave it, the more I cried; I went into a shell and became angry. I didn't know how to move at that time. However, what I did learn is that sometimes God will take you through some things that are meant to reveal your character. You may think you have it all together and know exactly what you're doing. God is kind enough to show that you still have some learning and growing to do. That's what he showed me.

What I had seen in that mirror wasn't good. When you get in certain situations, sometimes you can't see the areas where you still need growth and development. Sometimes a position of leadership feels like a burden. It can cause you to feel inadequate. I didn't always lean into God when I felt that way.

Where was God leading me?

I realized that I wasn't allowing God to control all areas of my life. I was in a bubble of just functioning. Even though I was praying, I had stopped allowing God to be God in my life. My concern was more fixated on others' feelings and thoughts rather than God and what I knew I should do. I had allowed the thoughts and feelings of others to become gods in my life. I depended on people to give a sense of gratification that only God could give.

What I have learned is that people will not always be there, but they will judge you and evaluate you from afar. I was headed down a road of destruction and didn't realize it. I was alive, but I wasn't living. I was just existing and going throughout my day. After I realized the impact it made, I couldn't believe "God allowed this to happen. He knew this would be the one that would take me out." I blamed Him for me putting others' in a place that He never meant for anyone to be in my life. But the hard truth was that I had done that myself, and He loved me enough to help me recognize that. If I hadn't realized that and allowed healing, true healing to take place; if I hadn't realized it was all a part of the bigger plan, then I would not be on God's plan for my destiny.

During this time, it was revealed that I did not trust God in those past trauma areas of my life. He exposed to me through this situation that I had not healed in those areas, and it was time. I was dealing with inadequacy of fulfilling the position. I had adopted negative things that others said and had not realized it. I wore past traumas like armor, and the burdens of them had gotten too much to bear. Somewhere along the way, I stopped casting them; I stopped casting my burdens unto God. I began to bandage my own wombs without allowing them to be cleaned. I wasn't taking advantage of the blessing that was before me. I began to wear leadership as a burden when it is a blessing.

God doesn't waste experiences. All things work together for the good of those who love God. God used my birthday experience to help me grow. There was some plucking and pruning that needed to take place in my life in order for me to assist others.

Own your feelings. Feel them. Sit with them, and seek to understand their core—the bottom of your trigger or response. Be honest with yourself. Don't allow yourself to become bitter; become better.

Most of us train ourselves to believe that blessings are a gift. When those same blessings cause pain or grief, we want to discard them. What I'd like to offer is that a blessing offers a mandate to grow. A blessing provides a call to excellence. There is development attached to blessings. When we ask God for a blessing, we are also asking to be called to excellence in an area so we can stretch. If we look at blessings that way, then we can have a different perspective on the things we experience.

Fifteen

Choose Thanks

How Gratitude Broke the Cycle of Abuse

MELINDA BURKHART

Have you ever felt crushed by fear? Not being able to take a full breath, muscles twitching, eyes darting all around to assess the scene? To see if you were safe? That was me growing up. It started at three years old. Well, that is my earliest memory of it.

As a child, I focused on surviving through the day. I did everything I could to stay hidden and not attract attention. My mom drank a lot, and she would get mean the more she drank. I didn't understand everything that happened then. I knew when I was seen, I got yelled at, made to feel stupid, or was a target, and it didn't feel good.

The person who targeted me most was my uncle, who was also my godfather, and it hurt! Then he would buy me ice cream and gifts when we went shopping, anything I wanted. It was so confusing, the mix of love with pain.

Then my family moved, and we were **the** Mexican family in a white neighborhood. We stood out. People noticed. After getting off the bus after school, a group of boys would chase me to beat me up. I learned to run fast, hide, and look over my shoulder. However, it really didn't matter if I looked over my shoulder, because my uncle was there in front of me. There was nothing I could do about that. He had warned me not to tell **or else**.

Other men who were neighbors got their hands on me as well. I felt so powerless, like a piece of meat.

Why me? Why was this happening to me? I am so scared! I can't get away. They are too big, too strong.

Over time I learned to stuff it down and leave my body when "bad things" were happening. I felt like I was two people: the me who lived inside and nobody ever saw, the one who screamed for help. The other me who was outside, the one people saw with the smile mask glued to my face. I always tried to make adults around me happy because some-how, I felt that would make me safer.

Books served as a magical escape, and I often immersed myself in science fiction. I would escape the world I lived, transporting my-self to far away planets. Helping others and saving the day in those wondrous stories, I was strong and without fear. My love for reading helped during school. I received good grades, and I loved learning and researching things.

My grades got me into a University of California college, where I continued my academic journey. I wasn't interested in going to col-lege, but my dad wanted me to go. He wouldn't let me say no. It was the expectation. So, I got a job to pay for school.

My mother's drinking increased. She would hide her glass of scotch in the fridge behind the half-gallon carton of milk, as if we wouldn't see it. At one point, she didn't recognize me. I didn't have my house keys and the front door was locked, so I knocked. She came to the door, asked who I was, said she didn't know me, and shut the door on my face. My body was shaking, my stomach churning.

My own mother doesn't know me! I am nothing!

I felt devastated. I moved out because I couldn't take it anymore. She yelled at me for moving out, but I had had enough. I felt like I was rotting to death from the inside. I needed out.

IN A DREAM STATE

At the university, I was in full force. I worked and went to class, ate, did homework, worked my second job, did more homework, slept, and repeated. I spread myself thin. I was stressed from school, having to pay my own way and trying to keep up with all my homework. I didn't realize how draining it was to ignore my feelings and pretend like everything was good. I stayed super busy to hide.

During my freshman year, I found a group on campus called Adults Molested as Children (AMAC). It was a free group for students, so I figured I would see what it was about. The meeting was held in a large room with chairs around a central open area. We would put our backpacks down near the door and put our keys in a bowl. We sat in a circle, and a therapist would guide the discussion.

After a few sessions, they took my keys away, and I got referred to a psychologist. I was deemed suicidal—they were right. I had been thinking of ways to kill myself and was zeroing in on one of two ways to do it. I was planning out both ways, determining when the best time of day was, etc.

This new psychologist was a lifesaver. I had been suffering from the same series of dreams every night for as long as I could remember. They started with me falling from my bed downward for miles before landing in a dark, deserted area with a pinpoint of light seen in the far distance. They ended with me dying from a huge fireball coming straight towards me through a wooded area. The new doctor specialized in dream therapy. It was a perfect match. I worked with him for months. I took incompletes in my classes, so I didn't have the stress of coursework on my plate as well. I focused on my mental health for the first time in my life.

The series of dreams finally ended. I remember the last night I had them. The fireball that always consumed me instead got smaller and smaller as it came towards me. It ended up a little speck of fire that I stepped on and mushed into the dirt.

That's it! I'm alive!

No more of those dreams! It was a blessing. It was weird. It was the start down a new road, a road that led away from the darkness. It was a long road, but one I was glad to find at that time. I later understood this to be divine intervention.

STARTING A NEW PATH

After six months, I returned to school and graduated with a bachelor's degree. I continued to see psychotherapists when I could afford it or when insurance covered it. I began working in a hospital as a therapy aide, and I received a master's degree and began working as a speech-language pathologist.

My first job out of college was in an acute hospital working on a brain injury unit. It was intense. It was stimulating. It was stressful. It brought me up against waves and waves of feelings of self-doubt.

Can I do this? Did I know enough to not kill somebody by accident? What was I thinking? Who am I to work here?

It was nerve-wracking work, and once again I shoved all those thoughts and feelings down. I retreated in my brain, and that is where I stayed. That was "safe". If I stayed in my brain, I didn't have to feel. I stayed on autopilot for quite a while, doing the expected. I had relationships that didn't last; I changed jobs; I moved often.

Then my dad ended up in hospice. He was dying from cancer. He hated hospitals, so he got well enough to come home, then he took a turn for the worse. A hospital bed was brought to his home, and he needed care. I knew how to care for someone in a hospital bed. I had experience helping nurses in the various hospitals and nursing facilities.

My mom couldn't afford a nurse to come help him, so I did it. I cared for him until he passed a month or so later. It was the most difficult thing I have ever had to do...to watch him die. To hear my mom wish that it was me instead of him on that bed. To be the only caregiver while that happened, the bed baths, dressing changes, everything. My brother would come to bring me coffee and give me a break. After drinking my coffee, I would go outside and run. I would run my hardest—as far and as fast as I could until I fell to my knees and cried it out. Then I would come back and do it again.

When my dad died, something in me shattered. I needed a change, away from that house, away from that city, so I moved to Hawaii and got a job. I made one-third of what I was earning in California, but I found a small room to rent behind someone's garage and made it work.

Eventually, I moved back to California to help my brother when Mom's health started to decline. I also started dating someone who didn't leave when I started to push.

He said, "I know what you're doing. It won't work."

We married and bought a house. We were happy. On the outside, things looked great! We both had good jobs, great careers, and a nice house in a desired area. On the inside, I was still miserable. I fought to get out of bed every morning.

Can I call in sick? One more snooze, I'll get up at the next alarm. Ugh, I can't move. I wish I could hide in bed all day!

I was overworked and hated my job. I cried on the way to work most days. I knew I needed a change. I had been going to therapy through insurance, and I still felt stuck.

BREAKING FREE FROM THE LOOP

After I saved some money, I began to investigate personal development. I took a twelve-week coaching program, two certificate courses on Neuro Linguistic Programming (NLP) , educational kinesiology courses, and several online coaching programs. I was looking for something, anything, to help me. These different courses had moved the needle a little, but there was still something huge, deep down that was not budging. I could feel it. It was like a hundred-pound weight in the middle of my belly.

I can't catch a break! I was miserable. When something good happened, my first thoughts were, *What's the catch? I can't trust this. When's the other shoe gonna drop?*

Lo and behold, the help I was looking for showed up via a side-business that I started in order to help my brother. It was an eight-week coaching program that came recommended from one of the founders of the business. I was hesitant to participate because I had been through so many years of therapy plus the coaching programs.

Why would this be any different? I thought.

Then I spoke to the coach who was leading the program. Something in his voice, and his conviction that this would work, motivated me to take the leap. I yearned for all the chaos I stuffed down deep inside me to finally be gone. I felt tired of the constant stress. Inside, I was begging for something to change because I knew in every cell of my body, I could no longer keep going the way I was. I was done. Living my life as a charade was a grueling endeavor. The constant surveillance of my surroundings and having eyes in the back of my head to feel safe exhausted me. I needed something to change. This course promised to get me unstuck, so I went for it. I'm glad I did because it changed every aspect of my life!

Through this course, I became aware of the constant loop of negative self-talk.

You're so f*ing stupid! Just die already! What a dumba%$!

It was awful. I am grateful to say this negative loop is gone! Through this deep, inner journey I learned to look with new eyes and become aware of patterns and behaviors I had never seen in myself. This new awareness allowed me to uncover and release hidden triggers that had sabotaged my interactions for years! I learned that I was projecting my unhealed wounds onto my husband, children, and friends. I had not realized how often I was doing that or how damaging it was to my daily interactions with everyone. I learned to forgive myself.

After this program, my relationships have improved, both at home and at work. Things that used to cause stress no longer do. Things I thought impossible are not so far away. It's like I found a magic door to a place where life is what I choose to make it. A place where I am able to see and be seen, to love and be loved in safety, without fear. I choose love. I choose peace. I choose gratitude.

> "Be thankful for what you have; you'll end up having more. If you concentrate on what you don't have, you will never, ever have enough." -Oprah Winfrey

I learned, and share with my coaching clients, the discovery of how we all have the ability to choose how we respond to things. That awareness was priceless to me. It opened not only my eyes but my heart as well. It opened me up to the possibility that others were being helpful, yet I wasn't seeing it. That life wasn't scary. I learned how to be in my physical body again, to be connected, to feel and recognize the feelings in my body. I learned that because bad things happened didn't mean God didn't exist. It didn't mean I was bad, and He was punishing me. In fact, looking back over my life, there were many things that fell magically into place. Things that I did not and could not have arranged.

Divine intervention?

What a game-changer for me! This new awareness allowed me to grow in love, compassion, and trust in myself as well as others. Your thoughts are your choice. Choose to be thankful every day.

One of the habits that helped most was a daily gratitude practice. Each morning before I started my day, I would write three things I was thankful for. You can try this too, and to supercharge this activity, Write three different things you are thankful for each day.

Watch how your world changes.

What I love to share is the ability to feel genuine happiness. To enjoy a true, from the heart, belly laugh and not fake it. I have not only broken the generational cycle of abuse, I now model as the active creator of my life for my children, grandchildren, friends, clients, and everyone I meet. I am so thankful to lead others through this journey, so they also can enjoy the deep sense of joy and peace that comes with it.

> "Give thanks in all circumstances; for this is God's will for you in Christ Jesus." 1 Thessalonians 5:18

Sixteen

Let Go and Let God

Rising Above Fear by Choosing Faith

JENNY LANG

A s I sit quietly on the couch and run my fingers across it, I feel the scratchy texture of the woven 1970s yellow and brown material, while gazing at all the people filling my small eleven-hundred-square-foot home.

In a blur of commotion, neighbors, family, and strangers surround us. It's hard to understand the chatter from anyone. My little eight-year-old self is in shock and confusion as to what just transpired, and I'm not sure how to comprehend the situation. I look around the room as if I'm still searching for the answers.

For a moment, I look over to my eleven-year-old brother sitting next to me evaluating his reaction, hoping for some type of guidance. His face doesn't move as he stares out. His expression is stoic and sad. He's in shock, too.

I see the priest walking through the front door and my mind wonders, *Why is he here? She already died.*

At that same moment, I really wasn't sure what death even meant. *Where did my sister go? Why was she not moving anymore? How did this all happen? She was smiling and laughing just hours before.*

Lights begin flashing outside the window, and what felt instantaneous, I could hear the paramedics come in the back door. Even though I couldn't see them, I could hear their boots pound as they walked across the linoleum floor, down the hallway, and into her room. I could hear the wheels of the stretcher as they came in. I could see the distress on my mother's face. I hated seeing her so sad. It felt like I was entrapped inside a bad dream and I couldn't wake up.

For my young mind, the emotions were there, but they felt trapped and I wasn't sure how to process them. I just stayed on that couch while the world moved around me. I felt safe there.

A few moments later the people started to get quiet and somber. I soon realized why as I began to hear the paramedics come back down the hall. It was the sound of the boots and rolling of the stretcher wheels. My mom began to sob. Even though I couldn't see what was happening, I knew she was being taken away.

Over the next hour or so, people began to leave. As the evening progressed, it became deep into the night, and we were left not knowing how to even proceed.

I don't even recall if I slept that night.

A LIGHT IN THE DARKNESS

My sister, Melanie, was fifteen years old when she died and had cerebral palsy. She was wheelchair bound, unable to vocalize words, but her smile and laughter lit up every room. Her soul was pure light and encompassed her disabled body, and it radiated so much love and joy. Even though she was immobile, she was beyond happy. Her beautiful long, dark brown hair was something my mother took great pride in braiding each day. The braids would flow along both sides of her face. Even though it was a younger girl's hairstyle, it fit her personality perfectly.

With cerebral palsy, came seizures. I remember many times seeing my mom run over to my sister when a seizure began. They are hard on anyone, even those who can move their body, but for someone with a crippled body, it was even more terrifying. My mother would hold her head to ensure she didn't get hurt, but also make sure she could breathe. These moments would stop me in my tracks, and as a young child, I wasn't sure what to do. These episodes were unexpected, and that alone scared me.

On that night in January 1985, one of those seizures ended up taking her life. It was the silent killer when she was sleeping in bed. My mother dedicated every day of her life to do everything she could to make sure my sister was safe, so this was something we never expected to happen.

Yet, that night changed our lives forever.

Losing a sibling is one thing, but now that I'm a mother, I cannot fathom how hard it was for my mother to lose a child. The love she has for her children runs deep into her soul.

For days after her passing, it was like I floated throughout life, with all the activities of her funeral, burial, and family gatherings. Everything felt emotional and overwhelming. I can recall sitting at church hearing the song, "Wind Beneath my Wings" and just sobbing, knowing she wasn't coming home again.

What unfolded in my home that night with my sister left an indelible imprint of fear in my life.

That fear crippled me and made an indelible mark long into adulthood.

FROM CRIPPLING FEAR TO LIGHT

For nearly a year after her death, I couldn't even walk down the hallway in my home without my mother by my side. I would cry and freeze just to go to the bathroom, which was next to my sister's room. I would literally run to a nearby room hoping the Grim Reaper wouldn't come and get me. My mother did all she could to comfort me through this time, even though I know she needed comforting too.

As years passed and our hearts healed, my mother would use signs from nature to help us all find comfort in losing our sister. When we'd have a thunderstorm and I'd get scared, she'd say, "That lightning is just Melanie flickering the light-switch in heaven. She's having the best time up there with the angels!"

She was right. Melanie found pure joy in the little things and would take any opportunity to lift her crippled hand to a light switch and turn it on. She'd laugh joyously every time. Those little comments from my mother helped me feel like Melanie was still around us—a happy guardian angel reminding us to find the little bits of joy in life.

For many years, my sister's bedroom door was left closed creating a museum out of the room she left behind. Even though there were five of us still living in our tiny home, that room was never occupied until I was in high school.

As I think back to the night my sister passed, I don't recall if my father came to the house. At this point in my life, I really didn't know who he was. My five older brothers had become my father figures, even to the point where they helped my mother financially by working as early as twelve years of age to fill the void of my father's lack of support.

Although he was seen as a timid and quiet man, my father was an alcoholic and had a broken heart that he couldn't get past, and I believe he used alcohol to fill that gap in his heart. He'd spend the little income he made as a shoe salesman. It was common for him to go to the downtown bar after work each day. This left my mother to raise us kids alone hoping that each day would be the day he would bring home some money to pay the mortgage and have a decent meal.

After fifteen years of a marriage filled with fear and anger, in 1977, my mother knew she needed to make the toughest decision of her life.

She received a letter from the mortgage company stating that the house was under foreclosure. She needed this home and had nowhere to go with seven children in tow. She had to stop hoping my father would change and do the one thing she had contemplated for years.

When she called the mortgage company, a representative stated, "If you don't pay, you will have to go into foreclosure and lose the house."

She had to put all fear aside, choose her children, and save our home, at the expense of her marriage.

She asked, "If I got divorced, would that help me save the house?"

The representative responded, "Yes, by doing this you may be able to stop this from happening."

She hung up and knew what she had to do.

Even though I know she loved my father, she chose us over him. She realized that she couldn't change him, and he wasn't the man she fell in love with. We all deserved better, even if better meant letting my father go.

Not until I was an adult, and after my father passed away in 2018, did she share the story of the day she and my father walked to the courthouse to finalize the divorce. She recalled how he walked slightly ahead of her, and as he opened the door to the building, he paused, turned to her and asked, "Are you sure you want to do this?"

She responded, "You leave me no other choice."

He didn't fight to change her mind, but instead turned back and proceeded to go into the courthouse.

THE SMALL EVERYDAY MIRACLES

As the years passed, I'd watch my mother work odd jobs and file for county grants to help pay the bills and for my sister's care. She put all humility aside and did everything possible to make ends meet and give us a happy and safe environment to live in. Yet, there were countless times I would see the worry on her face, tears shed, and how exhausted she was each day. Most days she worried how she'd be able to pay bills or feed us. She'd spend many late nights sewing to make our clothes or repair what we already had, as she knew she couldn't afford anything new. Local thrift stores and food shelves were such a blessing to us.

Even though there were many Christmas holidays with few gifts. My mom loved to be able to get gifts for each of us. She'd spend all night locked in her bedroom intricately wrapping each gift. This simple act was her way of allowing us to feel as much love and normalcy as possible.

As I look back, it was her unwavering faith and trust that God would get us through those dark days. We were always provided for, and God was carving the path for her. She had to believe this. Now as an adult, I reflect on how it perfectly unfolded. No matter how difficult life became, something always happened to allow us opportunities to save the house, get groceries and the needed medical care, or car repairs to keep us going. The right people and circumstances would just magically show up!

Each circumstance was a tiny miracle in itself.

In these uncertain times, I would often hear my mother say, "Let go and let God." She even had that quote framed or written throughout our home.

When I was young, I didn't understand the significance of this phrase, but now I do.

My mother taught me that if you allow fear to dictate your actions, you end up losing control and living in a place of fear instead of peace. By letting go, you allow life to unfold so small miracles happen each day.

This lesson played out over and over again throughout my life. The fear that held onto me wanted to control my life's outcomes and create a different future than what I experienced as a child. The life lessons continued to show up to remind me to let go. I used fear to put myself through college, which led to a corporate job with great success. Yet, it was far from peaceful. I wasn't truly letting go. Fear gripped me by creating debilitating anxiety, panic attacks, illnesses, and a very disconnected life.

This was far from the life I wanted to create.

The lesson of "Let go and let God" came back again in 2013 when I received a health diagnosis that knocked me off my feet and changed the course of my life.

Like my mother stepping into fear with faith, I left a twenty-year corporate career to listen to my calling and create my own practice as a Board Certified Health Coach. I believe that all of my life experiences were perfectly orchestrated for me to learn how to step into a life of serving others. My desire helps to lead others to their light, rediscover their true selves, and feel empowered to create a life of well-being and peace. Every part of my journey has led me to use my experiences, faith, and empathy to lead others on their healing journey. My hope is that my story will encourage them to find faith through fear.

These experiences and the lessons my mother learned became my own. It all prepared me to create a life full of peace and resiliency.

My sister's death and my father's absence was a lesson in trusting life and unconditional love.

It all propelled me forward and put me on a path to become the woman, wife, friend, and mother I am today. I realized that the darkest moments in life allow us to see the light on the other side.

That there is a balance between creating your life and allowing it to unfold as it should.

With letting go, I recognize the blessings by taking time to reflect each day with gratitude. This occurs in the simple moments or the intentional ones each morning when you wake up to a new day. My sister taught me that life can change in a single moment, so we need to love the moments we are given, no matter how typical the moment feels.

Yet, when life feels uncertain, scary, and I can't see the next step, I take time to go within by journaling, speaking to God through prayer, and listening to His message through meditation. I want to live each day in gratitude. I wake up thanking God for another day, to live with those I love, and be present enough to see miracles unfold.

I make the intention to tell my family I love them. I give gratitude for the things I have in life, and I take a minute before falling asleep to recount my day thanking God for everything, even the tough lessons from that day. If I feel fear creeping in, I remind myself, *You are always provided for. Everything will unfold as it should. Trust and have faith.*

Looking back, I realized that the fear wasn't something to run from, it was something to run towards. It wasn't a sign of being uncomfortable. It was a sign of something new. As Zig Zigler said, "F.E.A.R. has two meanings: 'Forget Everything and Run' or 'Face Everything and Rise.' The choice is yours."

I now choose to rise and live life knowing peace and joy are on the other side of fear.

Seventeen

Unexpected Rapids

Two Calls That Changed My Life

KERRIE GORDON

Throughout the thirty-five years of running my swim school business, I received thousands of phone calls ranging from, "When can I get my child into your schedule?" to "Can I book a pool party?" and "Are there any available spots in your summer adventure camp?" to "Are you hiring instructors?" and "Kerrie, 'Sally' didn't show up again; what sub should we call?"

Then there are the catch-your-breath calls like, "I have to tell you what my child did this weekend that helped him in a near-drowning situation. He is safe because of your program!"

Other calls, such as bank calls, extend your faith and prayers that things will work out. "Kerrie, we will float your payroll until tomorrow. Can you cover the twenty-five thousand by then?"

First, let's go back a bit. In 1986, as a twenty-one-year-old, I moved to Seattle to follow a dream I didn't realize I had. Starting my own business with a handful of swimmers, I grew my swim school business one swimmer at a time. My personal life changed as well. I got married and had six wonderful children. As they grew, so did the business. At one point, they each worked at the swim school in some capacity. My husband changed careers to help run it, truly making it a family business. We even had swimmers return to teach and later again as new parents with their own little swimmers.

Thirty-five years is a long time to devote your heart and energy to a growing family business. As a female entrepreneur, I weathered business growth challenges, constant staffing changes, the weekly payroll, and sometimes needed creativity to keep our doors open during the economic ups and downs. I struggled in the aftermath of 9-11 and the COVID-19 pandemic. However, through the years, I continued to push forward, training hundreds of instructors so hundreds of thousands of Seattle children could be taught to swim at our swim school. I could never have planned for what happened on December 13, 2021.

* * *

A few years earlier, Scott and I had relocated to Utah and took turns traveling back and forth to Seattle. One day, he felt the need to return to Seattle after getting home from a two-week stay. He followed an instinct to return, not knowing exactly why.

What Scott and our opening guard found on the pool deck that morning would stop both our hearts. Sheetrock was on the pool deck near a bank of floor-to-ceiling windows. At first, they couldn't figure out where it came from. They cleaned up the sheet-rock and prepared for the start of lessons. Feeling the need to check the windows again, Scott noticed the bank of floor-to-ceiling windows had shifted four or five inches at the building's window base and were now resting outside the window area on the dock running along the side of the building. The bottom of the window frame had shifted while the top had remained attached.

With so much of the pool's south wall being windows, Scott knew someone needed to check the area for safety before we started lessons. That's when he called me. When I answered, I could tell by the tension in his voice that something was wrong. His usual steady tone was shaky and laced with uncertainty.

"Kerrie, the pool windows are damaged and don't look safe. We need to cancel the morning swim lessons!"

Trusting what he saw wasn't safe for swimmers and staff, we called clients to reschedule their lessons. Most were still at home, some on their way, and others would soon arrive to see the damage. Knowing it was just the morning lessons seemed to calm my nervous heart.

His next call came at noon. "Kerrie, I can't get in touch with an engineer. We need to cancel lessons tonight and Tuesday morning, so I can get someone here to assess the damage."

Tuesday morning, he called again, "Kerrie, a city engineer, can be here Wednesday afternoon to inspect the damage."

I worried canceling lessons one week before a holiday break would be difficult for staff. I was also nervous we might not have enough money to cover three payrolls. My heart ached as the extended time out of the water would be hard for everyone. We were excited about the upcoming holiday break, but not when it was earlier than expected.

Since I was in Utah and Scott was in Seattle, the time between Tuesday and Wednesday at 4 p.m. seemed to halt. Each minute seemed to drag in slow motion. The floor in my kitchen and hallway were worn because of all my pacing. I paced, prayed, and prayed while I paced some more. Finally, it was Wednesday morning, and I watched the clock tick slowly.

When would Scott's call come? Can we salvage the last few days of the week or some of next week's pool parties?

At 5:20 p.m., the phone rang. It was Scott! *What would the news be? Would it be okay for us to resume lessons?*

Sadly, that call would never come.

As I answered Scott's call, my heart stopped, or at least skipped ten beats.

"Kerrie, are you sitting down? The news is not good."

My knees weakened, my hands went clammy, and my racing heart sank.

"We must close for the rest of the year and probably most of January. The building is unsafe to be in. The city engineer has closed all the businesses in the building."

I couldn't believe what I was hearing. When the engineer arrived, he instantly assessed the damage. Our pool space and the entire building were deemed unsafe, leading to its immediate evacuation.

For weeks after the devastating closure call, I felt like I was going down a river unprepared. The rapids were ready to take me under or knock me out of the raft. I could barely keep my bearings, let alone keep my 'nose up, toes up'.

This building closure call was worse than the news about closing our swim school for COVID-19. With the COVID-19 news, we felt our business would be closed for a few weeks. It turned out to be over three months, but with creative thinking and innovation, we survived.

Could we survive this building closure? There was no creative way to repair the south side of the building, and it had only been eighteen months since we reopened. Heavens, I was still picking up pieces and putting them together, working to cover payroll to retain our staff, and monitoring the health and safety of staff, swimmers, and parents.

We waited for news about the building from December 13, 2021, to March 16, 2022. Many days, I couldn't catch my breath. Crushing heartache took over; I could barely find the energy to move my arms and legs to go about my day. On other days, there was no plan but to wait—the ever-heart-wrenching wait to hear something.

As staff, parents, and swimmers waited for the news, we all hoped it would be another temporary closure. However, the call on December 13, 2021, marked the permanent closure of our thirty-five-year family business. Everything ended with that call. Our nest egg was broken. Our life savings was gone.

Our most difficult message was when we told our staff we couldn't reopen. They were like family, many working more than ten years for us. This devastating news hit everyone hard.

What would they do? Who could they serve? Swimmers and parents were also deeply disappointed they would no longer enjoy swimming lessons with us. We all felt a deep sense of sadness.

* * *

As I worked through the devastating end of our family business, I faced another life-altering challenge with a second phone call on March 16, 2022, at 8:30 a.m. As my phone rang, I saw on the screen the hospital was calling with my results. I suddenly had a sinking feeling the news would not be good. I took a few deep breaths, and before it went to voicemail, I swiped right. "Hello, this is Kerrie."

"Hi, Mrs. Gordon. I'm calling about your mammogram results. You need to come in again. The doctor would like you to have a second scan and a biopsy. Could I schedule you for that in the next few days?"

The next few days? I knew it was serious, and as I began to work out the scheduling with her, I realized this scan would not be the green light like in years past. After getting the second scan scheduled, I hung up the phone and took a few more deep, slow breaths to calm my racing heart. I tried to let the news settle. I didn't want to jump ahead of myself, but I could feel my brain going there—down the deep, dark spiral where I had been three months earlier with the first life-changing phone call regarding the swim school.

These two calls in three months challenged me, but upon reflection, I realize they helped me see the strength I have within me—a resilience to overcome a challenge by digging in and making it through as best as possible.

From March 16 to April 2, 2022, I was filled with the familiar, gut-wrenching anxiety. Each clock tick echoed loudly as I braced myself for what the doctor might say. When the office called with the test results, I reminded myself to take slow, deep breaths and remember that even though I couldn't control the outcome, I could prepare myself to go through it.

Hearing you have breast cancer is never easy to process. Navigating surgery, radiation, and the constant lack of energy on the heels of the permanent closure of a beloved family business was a challenge I thought for sure would overwhelm me.

Are we ever prepared for the call that changes our path and redirects us down a new one? I know I wasn't.

RIDING THE RAPIDS

In July 2024, I had an experience that helped me put these two life-changing events into perspective. It helped my brain and heart process what I learned after the calls came in.

It was my first experience running a local river. Our guide, Grace, and three other adventurers were in my raft. The river was running high and fast, with rapids, rock gardens, slow-moving eddies, and sweepers that threatened to push us out of the raft. I was so nervous and wondered if I could stay in the raft.

Grace gave us essential instructions on paddling and what commands to listen for. She reminded us to have fun and enjoy the trip; then she ensured our life jackets were a proper fit and emphasized, "Remember, if you find yourself out of the raft and in the water, 'nose up, toes up.'"

This phrase, "nose up, toes up," resonated within me, echoing what I needed to do during my unexpected challenges. Two phone calls—each bearing news that tossed me into life's turbulent waters—left me struggling to find which way was up. Thankfully, loved ones offered support, hugs, prayers, and their presence, which helped me regain my balance and get back in my raft.

Grace's confident instructions as we began our journey down the river instilled courage in my racing heart. Knowing how and when to paddle felt empowering. At first, paddling in sync was easy; the water and my nerves were calm. Then I saw the approaching rapids. My heart began to race, and I doubted my ability to navigate the difficult waters.

Can I paddle hard and long enough? I sat in the front right position of the raft and set the pace for the paddlers behind me. Could I set a pace that would help keep us going straight?

As I questioned myself, I heard Grace's voice, "Paddle forward!"

I thrust my paddle into the water and tried to set a good pace. Hearing splashing and the matching rhythm reassured me. Creating a rhythm felt great as we headed straight for the rapids.

With the first set of rocks and rapids close, I knew I couldn't stop the process—we were headed into the rapids. I needed to be present in the experience, paddling, not in a mental spin of doubt. I needed to paddle through and somehow enjoy the moment. Did I mention I forgot to breathe while we paddled through that set of rapids? During the first section, I held my breath as tightly as I held the paddle. As we navigated the next set of rapids, the first cold wave went right over the front of the raft and all over me.

"Wow, that's cold!" It caught my breath, and then I screamed, "Yay! I'm still in the raft!"

Continuing down the river, we paddled forward or backward as Grace directed, depending on the river and what we were trying to do. Nearing our third eddy—a calm spot by the riverbank—the current almost overtook us, but we dug deep and paddled hard. The determination that rushed through me felt amazing as we spun around to paddle up the river to get to the stopping spot to wait for the other rafts.

After battling the current, we sat and rested to catch our breath. Sitting there, I realized I had just paddled the river like I had faced the unexpected news from those two life-changing phone calls.

When the combined devastating news seemed overwhelming and spun me around, or almost took me under, I dug deep to make sense of it all. I relied on my inner strength and resilience to continue paddling through each day. I had been sucked under but found my way up when I was reminded that a business closing or a health challenge revealing itself does not make me a failure or not enough as a person.

Reflecting on the rapids, I see mental and emotional balance when I paddle forward. Watching for sweepers, the tree limbs that line the riverbanks that seem ready to knock me over or take me under, I realize I am capable, curious, and creative. I learned that if I get knocked out of the raft, I need to keep my 'nose up, toes up' and stay above the negative undertow that can overwhelm me.

I never expected to learn my life mantra of "Paddle Forward" on a river trip or to feel fear, joy, disappointment, success, exhaustion, and achievement from two phone calls. I still battle unexpected mental currents, rapids, and rock gardens of self-doubt, negative self-talk, and feelings that I'm not enough. However, adopting a different paddling strategy—time spent in nature and with family, reinforcing good mental fitness and self-care—will help me navigate through. I know this is where I learn, heal, and grow.

I know the importance of celebrating small and big wins as they come. I smile, reflect, and enjoy each moment, realizing that sometimes the best experience is sitting back, enjoying the journey, and expressing gratitude for the flow of life and where it's taking you.

Eighteen

Off With Her Head

Death to the Martyr in Me

RAVEN PETTY

How may I help you?

May I get you some water or a snack? Would you like me to rub your shoulders or get you an extra pillow? What about carrying your groceries? Or help with a project?

Since I was a kid, I've offered to help others. It feels like it's in my DNA.

As the oldest of three children, I grew up taking care of my younger brothers and stepped into a maternal role. In middle school, I graded papers for my teachers instead of participating in school activities like pep rallies and was voted Most Helpful. By seventeen, I had worked my way up from cashier to customer service manager at a local grocery store. When most teenagers were out with friends or participating in extracurriculars for college preparation, I was at work, providing service to others. That's another book, though.

Some may think I like attention or have a people-pleasing personality. Not at all. I was just born to serve—much like a born musician plays or a born athlete competes.

What I didn't realize was that serving others chipped away at my soul. Over the years, each action for someone else felt like one ice pick stab at a time. The need to serve others became an alternate identity, like an arch nemesis, and also my mission in life. Make others as comfortable and happy as possible.

As I entered my mid-thirties, something inside me changed. By this time, my son was in high school. My ex-husband and I had started divorce proceedings. Plus, I was in a new relationship, and we were down to one income. I worked two jobs just to pay the bills. Then there was laundry, house cleaning, grocery shopping, errands, and little emergencies like car repairs and doctor visits. On the bright side, I had a loving partner and son, supportive friends, job security, and a dedicated family.

I had never felt more alone. Something snapped.

Isn't this what I'm supposed to do? I help others. This is serving others. Right?! These thoughts swirled through my head daily. I was completing my mission, and yet I felt hollow, drained, resentful, angry, invisible.

Mothers sacrifice themselves to provide for their families. They cook and clean, work inside and outside the home, pick up and drop off, pay bills, shop, attend events, and keep everything running without obstacles. They can handle anything.

Loving partners make time for their partner. They maintain good hygiene and wear sexy clothes and makeup. They laugh at every joke. Compliment their partner on how they look. Buy little presents to show appreciation. They hold space on tough days and listen.

Women aren't afraid to hustle. They're strong, independent, self-sufficient. They have to work twice as hard because men often make a higher salary and have more opportunities for promotions. Despite society's strongholds, women stand on their own because the well-being of everyone in the home, and the rest of the world, depends on it.

Bull shit.

These are the beliefs that society, Southern culture, and family programmed into me. From my family's perspective, it's the way all women in my family have lived. We provide for others and stay so busy you don't have time to feel anything for more than a few seconds. Shake it off and focus on the work. These beliefs also encourage women to not ask for help or delegate—and never speak up for what you really want. A higher salary, better job, less selfish people in your life, or just a day to do nothing without feeling guilty.

WHAT IS MARTYRDOM?

Merriam-Webster defines martyrdom as, "The suffering of death on account of adherence to a cause and especially to one's religious faith." Modern definitions have evolved into the martyr complex, which means to sacrifice your needs and wants in order to serve others, including children, a spouse, or job. These martyrs often feel powerless and resentful due to others' demands.

When did my innate desire to serve transform into suffering and dying in order to keep everyone else alive and happy?

I was doing everything I had always done, but it started to hit me in new ways. When others needed me, they felt like a leech. I couldn't understand why everyone else wouldn't do all the things I did every day. Over time, I became exhausted, developed a drinking problem, had spells of depression, cried, lashed out, and forgot important things. Even today I don't remember much from that time.

I also realized those years of service had sacrificed my well-being, and I needed to take action or I was going to have a stroke or heart attack. One day I looked in the mirror at my sunken, dark eyes and dry wrinkles and said, "Enough."

LEARNING A NEW LANGUAGE CALLED SELF-CARE

Changing something overnight doesn't work, so I knew my first step was to reconnect with my higher power and my higher self. I began to pray, meditate, journal, read devotionals, pull cards, and spend time outdoors in nature hiking and swimming. These practices helped me realize I needed to invest time, energy, and money in my needs. It was time to serve myself.

Next came self-care, but what does that term mean? During childhood, conversations about money and finances caused stress and domestic fights in my house, so I learned at an early age you don't buy things for yourself or ask for anything you don't need. As an adult, I learned to ease these restrictions and enjoy some treats such as a long vacation. However, I still felt a void. My soul ached for something just for me.

One evening, my partner encouraged me to subscribe to a beauty box that I had talked about for two years. Yes, that's how long it took me to spend fifteen dollars a month on myself. This beauty subscription created a surge of empowerment that led to spending more money on self-care and introduced me to the possibility that I could level-up my situation. The next investments included books, hobbies, workouts, clothes, jewelry, lingerie, monthly massages, and personal development workshops.

Getting out of the house became a form of self-care as well. I already worked from home, so the 2020 quarantine was no big deal. By the time the pandemic set-in, I had a renewed sense of courage and freedom. That year, I even left my husband and dog at home, drove seven hours, and enjoyed four nights at the beach by myself. Highly recommend it. When I couldn't find anyone to hang out with in my hometown, I took myself to lunch or the movies. Going to the movies and enjoying your own snacks provides a refreshing break if you've never tried it.

The largest investment I made in myself, aside from college, was also in 2020 when I decided to get certified as a health and life coach.

For a couple of years prior, I considered a career change, and in 2020, I saw so many people suffering. Once again, I felt called to help, but this time was different. I was an evolved version of myself who had developed boundaries with other people and could combine all of these skills to serve others in a healthy way.

Going back to school was terrifying, but one morning my eyes popped open at five a.m., my inner voice screaming at me to enroll. Best decision ever. Now my career could give me the ability to start my own business and leave corporate life while satisfying the innate desire to serve. By choosing a career that was in service, I was able to separate my desire to serve from my personal life and experience the best of both worlds.

THE DEATH OF MARY MARTYRDOM

At times, transformation is hard. The process can feel draining, frustrating, and never-ending. We can also become addicted to personal development, so it's important to find balance between accepting that we are whole and complete and recognizing areas that may need improvement.

Thich Nhat Hanh said, "Thanks to impermanence, everything is possible. Life itself is possible."

Impermanence means nothing stays permanent. Therefore, we will change and not remain the same. What if in order to create happiness and feel gratitude, we have to let go of everything we've been taught and know to be true? We have to evolve into newer versions of ourselves—or at least accept we are going to change because that's the nature of life. We become versions who have more resilience and adaptability to the world around us. Everything around us changes, so why wouldn't we?

Saying no has never been a problem. Offering to help has been the issue. When someone shares a problem, I want to help find a solution. When I see someone in need, I offer help. That had to stop.

I remember one of the first times I did not offer to help. My partner had a long day at work and asked me to run an errand for him. I said, "No, I'm super busy today."

Side note: Just because someone works from home, it doesn't mean they have free time to do chores and errands or have free time for other people.

Instead of saying, "Sure!" and figuring out how to add it to the to-do list, I started suggesting that others tend to themselves. Words cannot express how empowering this felt. Every time I didn't offer to help or said no, my body would get warm and my heart would pound out of my chest. My adrenaline rushed due to fear and excitement. Saying no became a daily goal. Each time, my body beamed with pride for standing up for myself and letting go of the guilt by not being in service.

Over time, saying no evolved into asking for help instead of doing everything. I asked for help with chores and cooking. I asked for back rubs. I started ignoring the subtle hints people would drop before they asked for a favor or expressed distress. "What can I do to help?" became "What have you done to solve this problem?"

One of the biggest actions was taking Wednesday nights off from everything and going to bed at 8 p.m. To this day on Wednesdays, I say goodnight to the family, go into the bedroom, close the door behind me, and do a little dance. I might as well drop the mic. What I call the "mid-week reset" has been a weekly routine for years.

This is what boundaries look like. Boundaries are how we show others to treat us. Boundaries are what we allow and don't allow, and they change. What was okay ten years ago may not be okay now, and that is okay. Much like with life, our boundaries change as we learn and step into the person we want to be. We must recognize when those boundaries have been crossed and stand up for ourselves.

WHAT NOW?

One of the biggest challenges of killing the martyr in me was how it affected my relationships with other people. In short, it created and still creates conflict and distance. My husband was pretty shocked when I started not doing things or suggested he take care of it. With friends, I would often go hours or days of not responding to texts because I wasn't interested in the conversation. Sometimes I just don't feel like talking, and let's get real, we all need to put our damn phones down. Other people started to notice the shift and commented on how I seemed happier. Others I don't talk to anymore, especially people who feed off of negativity and ask too much of me. Some have rejected me because we don't connect as well. That's okay too.

Instead of dwelling on the loss, I feel gratitude for all of those people no longer in my life because they created space for new people in my life. People who are creative, strong, vulnerable, ambitious, fun, and happy. Many are women. For this "guy's girl," that's a big change in energy. Each person has their own boundaries, and we go at our own pace. There are no expectations or judgments. In my heart, I know that without removing former friends and colleagues from my life, I wouldn't have the support group I have today.

These new boundaries also allow me to honor what I need. They encourage me to spend time with people who accept me just as I am. They allow me to stay in integrity with myself to avoid overextending my energy. In turn, these boundaries have allowed me to have more fun and healthier relationships with my friends, family, and colleagues. There is no longer resentment or codependency. There is peace.

All of this work led to the ability to develop a self-awareness that allows me to check-in on myself throughout the day and adjust my schedule as needed. Instead of catering to everyone else, I ask myself, How am I feeling right now? What do I need?

Most days, we experience the weight of our to-do lists leading to survival mode, shifting from one gear to the next without stopping.

When we take a moment to ask these questions, we give ourselves permission to think and feel. In doing so, we may realize we need something specific such as a quick walk, a glass of water, or a friendly shoulder to cry on. Even in short bursts, it's better to experience our feelings rather than bury them in an endless to-do list.

Plus, this enables us to devote dedicated time and space to things we love. Spending time outdoors, working on my business, meditation, painting, movies, music, and taking long drives all top my list. When we feel our best, others around us benefit. They feel our energy and may relax a little more. Life is just one big energy vortex that affects everyone.

Possibly the biggest lesson I learned was that no one else is going to take care of me in the way I need. That is my responsibility. Daily doses of joy are necessary. Taking time to rest charges my introvert batteries. Boundaries set the bar for what is accepted.

That is the freedom to choose my needs over the needs of others. By feeling my best, I serve in new ways without sacrificing my livelihood and well-being.

You have the same freedom. You have the same choice. Choose you.

Nineteen

From Burnout to Breakthrough

Empowering Tools Every Women Needs Now

LYNN DUDLEY

The cold, hard slab of the bathroom floor felt oddly refreshing against my sweaty skin.

It was safer down here. If the Earth was going to swallow me up, at least I was already on the ground—a shorter distance to my death. Perhaps sparing me a few seconds of agony on the way out.

Time stool still for me. I saw it pass for others, but not for me. I was stuck. Or maybe I was lost. Either way, I couldn't move forward. Each day was only about getting to the end of it just existing, not really living. Slowly drowning.

Don't worry. My flirtation with the dark side of the mind was a blessing in disguise. The twisted musings of my hijacked brain are firmly in my rear view mirror.

"Amy" I called her, and to all the Amy's out there, I apologize. I decided to give her a name about two years into her regular visits. In retrospect, her visits should have been predictable because they were somewhat cyclical. At the time however, they seemed random, annoying, and intrusive.

To the outside world, I was doing just fine. My pleasantly robotic, "I'm fine." was the standard answer to the question we so often ask each other. My guess is I wasn't the only unfine-fine person out there. Amy had convinced me I was the only one.

Being anything but fine didn't seem like a viable option for me. I didn't have time for less than perfect.

I was juggling family responsibilities and a successful career in medicine. Like many working moms, I wore my superhuman ability to handle **anything** as a badge of honor. In between the doing, there was also the thinking. There was never a moment when my brain was off duty. Like many moms, I was also the thinker, the planner, the plotter, with a constant scroll of to-dos playing in the background of my life.

The constant juggling, doing, and thinking eventually burned me out.

Burnout is a feeling many women know all too well. The sneaky thing about burnout is that by the time you realize you're burned out, it's too late. So many women push through their days, often feeling tired, overwhelmed, and frustrated. Then one day, they can't push through anymore.

For me, the impact of burnout was both physical and mental. My body was tired and not just a normal tired. The kind of fatigue that prevents you from doing normal things without paying a price. I had a certain reserve of energy, beyond which there was no pushing. Some days my energy tank held only enough fuel to get me to the grocery store and back. If I had no choice but to push myself beyond my limits, I would sometimes pay the price by feeling physically ill afterward.

The mental part of burnout was even worse.

My burnout often manifested as anxiety. Anxiety is something that most people think they understand. Unless you've actually experienced it, it's hard to know what it feels like. My experience with anxiety is unique to me, and my description is not meant to define, explain, or diagnose anyone else's symptoms or experiences.

There are different types of anxiety and different manifestations and symptoms that encompass a wide spectrum.

First, a brief tour of your brain.

Anxiety or even panic can occur when your brain is hijacked by a hypervigilant fear response, orchestrated by a region in the brain called the amygdala, so I thought "Amy" was a charming name for my anxiety.

Amy does a really good job of protecting us from actual threats. On the other hand, when she gets stuck in fight-or-flight, she can easily overtake the logical, rational-thinking part of the brain. The physical symptoms of a fear response can mimic many other conditions—shortness of breath, rapid heart rate, sweating, nausea, chest pain, dizziness or light-headedness, numbness, or tingling sensation.

The most troubling symptom of anxiety for many people is the sense of impending doom, danger, or imminent death. That's what anxiety felt like for me.

Like slowly drowning.

Only nobody knew I was drowning.

And I didn't know why I was drowning.

Like an uninvited guest, Amy often appeared in my life without warning.

When she visited me, breathing felt like a luxury just beyond my grasp. She came and went at will—at work, at home, during the day, or at night. Sometimes she only stayed for a few minutes, but sometimes she stayed for a few days or longer.

Logic left the party when Amy came around me. I wasn't **actually** dying. My lungs worked just fine, but Amy could convince me otherwise.

In the midst of her grip, the next day, or even the next moment, never seemed guaranteed.

Amy and I had an on-again/off-again relationship for a few years. I denied her existence to myself and, of course, to others.

There were even spans of weeks or months that she didn't visit at all. When she returned, each visit seemed worse than the last. So much so, dread became my constant companion in between her visits. Peace was increasingly elusive.

There must be a reason this is happening to me. There must be a way out of this pickle I find myself in. This can't be how I'm meant to live the rest of my life.

Hey logic - are you still in here?

You see, logic rules my day job.

As a functional medicine practitioner for the past two decades, I've treated thousands of patients using cutting-edge tools designed to uncover the root cause of their symptoms. The majority of my patients are female, middle-aged, and often working moms with children.

With so many patient encounters under my belt, it's easy to see shared patterns and commonalities.

Patterns I ignored in myself.

A major tenet of functional medicine is that the body's systems are all interconnected. No one system operates in isolation, and rarely is only one system to blame for a person's symptoms.

I hear their stories every day—insomnia, fatigue, menstrual symptoms, irritable bowel symptoms, headaches, mood issues, headaches. Her doctor runs basic tests and tells her she's fine, but offers a prescription nonetheless.

She's looking for real answers, a deeper dive into the root cause of her challenges.

I'm the functional medicine detective she's desperately hoping can solve her case. The tools of my investigative process are comprehensive blood work, saliva, and stool testing.

An equally important investigative tool is just listening. I listen to her story, and sadly, I am often the first practitioner who has ever fully listened to it.

The divorce, the special needs child, the demanding boss, the neglectful husband, the ailing elderly parents, the lost job, the financial worries, the childhood trauma, the relentless travel schedule...the endless stories. We all have a story.

Then there are the concerns about her own health symptoms. Compounding her frustration is that her concerns are often ignored, dismissed, or masked over with offers of prescription quick fixes.

She's a unique puzzle. Her genetics, her upbringing, her diet, lifestyle, and habits, her environment, her stressors, her exposures—they all form the complexities of her case. Her symptoms are just the clues.

In my experience, there are four major causes of the health havoc in her life:

Hormonal imbalance: The delicate, cyclical dance between estrogen and progesterone commonly becomes disrupted as a result of chronic stress and burnout. This can lead to menstrual irregularities, heavy bleeding, menstrual cramps, breast tenderness, moodiness, including depression or anxiety, weight gain, and bloating, which is most pronounced a week or so before the menstrual cycle starts.

Autonomic nervous system (ANS) dysregulation: As the maestro of your sympathetic (fight-or-flight) and parasympathetic (rest and digest) reactions, the ANS commonly becomes dysregulated due to chronic stress. The constant demands on our time and never-ending responsibilities shouldered by many women warriors leave us in fight-or-fight too often or for too long. The consequences of this constant sympathetic overdrive are felt in every other system in your body. In fact, medical research estimates that as much as ninety percent of all illness and disease is stress-related! (Liu YZ, Wang YX, Jiang CL. "Inflammation: the common pathway of stress-related diseases". *Front Hum Neurosci.* 2017).

Microbiome dysbiosis: The trillions of microorganisms comprising your gut microbiome are under constant assault and frequently tilted to a dysbiotic state. The most obvious outcome of imbalanced gut flora are gastrointestinal symptoms such as bloating, gas, diarrhea, pain, constipation, or heartburn. The complex relationship between your gut and your brain via the vagus nerve also leads to further ANS dysregulation.

Metabolic dysfunction: Insulin resistance and blood sugar fluctuations are common yet insidious culprits behind symptoms such as fluctuating energy levels and fatigue, weight gain or weight loss resistance, anxiety, headaches, and hormone symptoms, to name a few. In addition, insulin resistance is at the root of heart disease, diabetes, certain cancers, and Alzheimer's disease.

My job is to put the pieces of the puzzle together for my patients, and connect the dots from their symptoms to the source.

The good news is once you know your body, you can own your health. The tools of recovery often involve a recalibration of the foundations of good health.

The biggest transformations I've seen in my practice revolve around using food as medicine, prioritizing sleep and body movement, and consistently implementing tools to reset and maintain a healthy nervous system response.

Armed with eye-opening discoveries about themselves and empowered with the tools they need to thrive, my patients often transform before my eyes.

I don't fix my patients. I just light their path.

*Ohhhh, I finally get it. My purpose here is to figure out what's going on with **me** so that one day I can show others the way! Amy is not the enemy afterall; she's the messenger. Trying to avoid her and ignore her only made her speak louder.*

Finally, logic rejoined the party.

I still remember that day like it was yesterday. A panic attack in the middle of the workday that literally brought me to my knees.

Something about that day was different. Like the cliche, it was like a light-bulb went off, lighting the recesses of my brain that had been living in Amy's shadow for so long.

People in the medical profession often make the worst patients. I still find it ironic that my job was and is to help people with exactly the same issues I had, but I either couldn't or wouldn't admit that I needed the same help.

That day was a turning point for me. I rolled up my sleeves and got to work as the detective on my own case.

I found that my main problem was quite severe hormonal imbalance due to perimenopause. Turns out, too much estrogen was triggering my anxiety and disrupting my sleep. Digging a little deeper, I found that chronic stress had negatively impacted my cortisol, which in turn was making it more difficult to keep my blood sugar stable. Add to that, sensitivities to gluten and dairy had disrupted my gut microbiome, leading to fatigue, headaches, and eczema.

I finally solved my own puzzle.

Making the diet and lifestyle changes was easy for me. Taking some supplements was a piece of cake. I would have walked over hot coals in order to feel like myself again.

The harder part was dealing with my stress, and recognizing that my failure to deal with it was most likely the lynchpin that led to my burnout and downward spiral.

I knew my nervous system needed some tender loving care, but how to do it?

I read, I researched, I tried it all.

I found one of the most effective and well-researched tools for stress regulation is meditation.

Skeptical but desperate, I took the leap of faith and became a twice-a-day meditator. I am convinced to this day that meditation was the most impactful thing I implemented.

I also relearned how to breathe correctly, incorporating various breathing techniques throughout the day designed to access my parasympathetic nervous system and create signals of calm.

Regular therapy visits were a must for me. Turns out, your nervous system holds on to old stuff, too. Even stuff you may not think of as a big deal. Sometimes the simple act of talking about the old stuff can signal your nervous system to let it go and know that everything's okay.

I filled my stress management toolkit with techniques I could pull out whenever needed. Some were almost too simple—like watching something funny on television that would make me laugh. Others took more time and effort—like regular massage and acupuncture. All were meant to recalibrate and de-excite my overstimulated nervous system.

Turns out, everything I needed to recover from burnout was in my hands.

Turns out, your body and brain have a remarkable capacity to heal once you figure out what it needs and provide it.

Within a few months of implementing all these changes, Amy stopped visiting.

I don't miss her, but I am grateful for our time together.

I never thought I'd say that.

Being several years removed from my relationship with Amy has given me clarity and perspective.

The need to be unflappable kept me quiet. The stigma around mental health issues is still pervasive. My profession magnified my vulnerabilities.

I hope my cautionary tale spurs others to reach for the life ring buoy faster.

You don't have to suffer in silence.

You don't have to settle for just being fine.

Seek out functional medical professionals who will listen to your story, run the right tests, and empower you with the tools you need to own your health.

Don't wait until you crash and burn to ask for help. Find someone with a flashlight to light your path.

Stock your stress management toolkit with things that work for you, and use them every day.

Make friends with your feelings, even the unpleasant ones. Try giving them a silly name. They are often our best teachers and messengers.

Above all else, hold on and have faith. A breakdown often happens right before a breakthrough.

Twenty

Grace and Gratitude

What Stage 4 Cancer Taught Me About Living Life to the Fullest

LAURA MCKAIL

For years, I buried my soul in the relentless pursuit of perfection, sacrificing my peace and happiness in the quest for professional validation.

Hi, my name is Laura, and I'm a recovering perfectionist and workaholic. There must be a support group somewhere out there for people like me, I thought.

I spent years tirelessly climbing the corporate ladder, chasing achievements at work, and seeking validation for a job well done. With a relentless work ethic and commitment to my career, I had a work-before-play mentality and a never-ending to do list. Execution and delivery ahead of schedule were second nature to me. Can you relate?

Is this really what I want? What am I missing out on? I would hear these quiet whispers in my head.

As my responsibilities at work grew, so did my stress levels. I sacrificed my self-care, precious time with family and friends, and personal happiness all in pursuit of success. I was too lost in the endless whirlwind of daily tasks and responsibilities at work to notice. I was happy and ignorant of everything I was missing in life.

On a quiet and dark winter morning, my bare feet slipped out of bed and hit the cold floor, while at the same time my iphone would light up to show emails coming in from my colleagues across the globe. I found my way to the kitchen and as the aroma of coffee filled the air, I ventured down the hall to my home office. Still in my pajamas and before I even finished that cup of coffee, my fingers hit the keyboard rapidly firing out emails. Lunch time arrived before I had even dressed for the day. I skipped meals while my stomach growled and rumbled, but I didn't notice as I was in a constant barrage of responding to emails and jumping on conference calls. I relied on another cup of coffee to get through that afternoon slump. I often worked late into the evening and on weekends. Leftover meals in the microwave, quick snacks, and pizza for dinner became my mainstream meals.

Just another typical day at work.

Self-care became the lowest of priorities on my to-do list. I neglected sleep, exercise, relaxation, hobbies, and following my passion, leading to physical and mental exhaustion. I lived with this constant internal pressure to accomplish task after task, which slowly eroded every ounce of my well-being. Ultimately, in my quest to meet every single demand and expectation that came my way, I sacrificed everything that brought balance and happiness to my life. I was lost and didn't even realize it.

How did I end up here?

Have you ever lost yourself somewhere along the way? Maybe for you it wasn't your job, but something else. I wonder why so many of us put ourselves last on the to do list. I know I'm not alone in this behavior.

Outside of work, my world felt empty and quiet. When the cell phone texts no longer came in from friends with that familiar buzz, the silence became haunting and left me feeling empty. I had canceled too many gatherings, so my friends gave up on me, and those social invitations that had once filled my calendar were just distant memories. I missed out on precious time with family because I was too busy, or honestly, just too exhausted. I felt isolated and exhausted. Talk about FOMO (Fear of Missing Out). Can you think of a time when you felt that way? It feels pretty crappy, to be honest.

I was missing out on so much. The vibrant sunsets I never paused to admire, the laughter of loved ones I never heard, the gentle touch of hand went unnoticed–so many moments slipped by, unappreciated. I rushed from one obligation to the next and in my tunnel vision, I missed the simple, profound joys that make life meaningful. I never realized the true essence of living lies in some of those fleeting, beautiful moments.

Then out of nowhere I was confronted with news. News that would forever change the trajectory of my life.

I was diagnosed with stage four metastatic breast cancer. A diagnosis for which there is no cure. It is considered treatable, but not curable, with a median survival of two to three years from the time of diagnosis.

This was a huge wake up call that hit me like a ton of bricks. This life-altering news jolted me into the profound realization that life is fragile and fleeting. When faced with the stark reality of my diagnosis, it became obvious that the relentless pursuit of professional success had robbed me of the simple, irreplaceable joys that make life worth living. In the face of such a grave prognosis, I came to understand the futility of my relentless pursuit of perfection and the superficial rewards of overwork.

The questions I would ask myself. *Was I being true to myself in the way I was living my life? What changes can I make?*

The cancer diagnosis reminded me that life is meant to be lived. I no longer wait for a special occasion to drink from the fancy wine glasses or pull out the good china. I take time to stop and watch the sunrise. I know the to-do list will always be there, but it's more important to spend time making memories with friends and family and practice self-care. This realization has brought more meaning and joy to my life. In a way, the cancer diagnosis awakened me to a new appreciation for life and living my best day every day.

I wish I could have shared these sentiments with my former self, years before the cancer diagnosis. I wish I could shout it from the rooftops so everyone who has lost themselves along the way could realize how much more there is to life.

It's never too late to change. I thought to myself.

What would make me truly happy?

I did some soul searching and embarked on a journey of self-discovery and healing, which included the following main components. Collectively, these practices have brought me a profound sense of inner peace, grace and gratitude:

I now practice mindfulness and meditation. I am fully present in conversations with others, and I put down the cellphone and turn off the television so they have my full attention when we talk. Throughout the day I make a conscious effort to stay present and engage with my surroundings. Meditation and yoga help keep my head focused on the present moment. Sometimes I'll take my camera and venture off to photograph nature. Other days I focus on journaling and writing. I end each day by watching the sunset, allowing myself to be fully present and engaged in the moment. It's a mindfulness practice that also helps me reflect on the day, my life, and prioritize what truly matters.

Every day I live with grace and gratitude, and self-care is now at the top of my to-do list. My life has transformed into a vibrant, sensory-rich experience, where self-care is now a way of living. I make time for regular exercise and have adopted a healthier diet. I now have hobbies that bring me joy. Self-care is now much more intentional. I go for walks on the beach, not as I used to in a hurried pace to rush back home to whatever was next on the schedule for the day, but at a leisurely pace so I take it all in with all of my senses.

I seek out support and encouragement when I need it and have realized the importance of community. I reconnected with loved ones and rebuilt my social support network. I am no longer defined by my work or my accomplishments, but by the depth of my relationships and the joy I find in everyday life.

I have also found ways to incorporate grace and gratitude into my daily routines, and I have developed habits that reinforce a lifestyle of gratitude. I keep a daily gratitude journal that reminds me of the small and often overlooked blessings in my life. I embrace each day with a renewed sense of grace and gratitude, cherishing the moments that truly matter. This practice also helps me slow down and appreciate every day.

Creating a gratitude journal provided an easy way to enhance my well-being and cultivate a positive mindset. It's a simple practice and easy to start as a daily habit. The first step was to find a journal I could carry with me in a color or pattern that spoke to me. I prefer a physical journal that I can take with me to my favorite quiet spot out in nature. I've also gotten into a regular daily pattern of writing, which helps keep me consistent. Sometimes I write something simple, such as gratitude for the moment. When I'm really stuck on what to write, I often just start with "Today, I am grateful for...," and I often find it inspiring to go back to past entries in the gratitude journal to remind myself of all the things that I'm truly grateful for in my life.

Each day comes with a renewed sense of grace and gratitude. This shift in perspective has led me to prioritize meaningful connections, self-compassion, and the simple joys of daily life, finding solace and strength in the beauty of the present moment. It took a diagnosis of stage four metastatic breast cancer to help me realize that life is precious and we should embrace each day with grace and gratitude.

Now a typical morning begins with the light from the sunrise filtering down the hallway. I enjoy a few moments of quiet reflection and step out onto my balcony with an ocean view and take in the salty air. I walk or run near the beach for about thirty minutes to clear my head and come home to a balanced breakfast with fruits and grains, savoring each bite, feeling it nourish my body. I go to the gym at least four times a week to strengthen my body, which I follow with a restorative yoga class, giving me balance.

I cherish the laughter shared with loved ones, the warmth of a hug, and the quiet moments of reflection that nourish my soul. Each day is a precious gift, a chance to create beautiful memories and be present in the lives of those who matter most. I've learned to celebrate the small victories, savor the beauty in the mundane, and find strength in vulnerability. It has taught me that true fulfillment comes not from external achievements but from the love we give and receive, the connections we forge, and the moments of grace we allow ourselves to experience.

What about you? What small steps can you take today?

It took a life-altering diagnosis to help me realize that life is precious, and we should learn to embrace each day with grace and gratitude. Don't wait for life to hit you with a huge wake-up call. It's never too late to start living your best life, filled with purpose, gratitude, and unwavering hope.

This Book Gives Back

For *Heal to Lead: Stories to Turn Your Wounds Into Wisdom* Volume Two, we give one-hundred percent of all net proceeds to the National Alliance on Mental Illness (NAMI), which has hundreds of locations throughout the United States.

NAMI is a nonprofit organization dedicated to improving the lives of individuals affected by mental illness. Founded in 1979, NAMI advocates for better mental health policies, raises awareness about mental health issues, and provides support to families and individuals navigating the complexities of mental illness. The organization strives to create a more informed society that understands mental health challenges and reduces the stigma often associated with them.

NAMI offers programs designed to support individuals living with mental health conditions and their families. Through initiatives like NAMI Family-to-Family, NAMI Basics, and NAMI Peer-to-Peer, the organization provides crucial education and resources. These programs empower participants by offering information about mental health conditions, effective communication strategies, and coping skills. Additionally, NAMI's helpline serves as a vital resource, connecting individuals with local services, support groups, and community resources, thereby ensuring that no one navigates their journey alone.

In addition, the organization engages in legislative efforts to promote policies that enhance mental health care access and quality. NAMI's campaigns address critical issues such as mental health parity, access to treatment, and the need for increased funding for mental health services. By working alongside policymakers and other advocacy groups, NAMI aims to create systemic changes that improve the mental health landscape in the United States and beyond. Their efforts help to ensure that mental health care is treated with the same importance as physical health care.

Through these initiatives and events, NAVI creates public awareness about mental health issues. By hosting events like Mental Health Month in May and National Suicide Prevention Month in September, NAMI encourages communities to engage in conversations about mental health. These campaigns aim to dispel myths, foster understanding, and promote the importance of seeking help. For more information, visit https://www.nami.org/.

The authors of this book have created a digital workbook to accompany this book. It includes valuable tools to support your own journey. You'll find activities to enhance creativity, meditations to ease stress, journal prompts to encourage gratitude, and communication tools to deepen your relationship to others. To download the free workbook, visit https://ravenandgrace.com/healtolead2.

www.ingramcontent.com/pod-product-compliance
Lightning Source LLC
Chambersburg PA
CBHW051313120626
46547CB00015B/2214